Terence, Arthur Sloman

P. Terenti Adelphi

With Notes and Introductions - Intended for the Higher Forms of Public Schools

Terence, Arthur Sloman

P. Terenti Adelphi
With Notes and Introductions - Intended for the Higher Forms of Public Schools

ISBN/EAN: 9783337157883

Printed in Europe, USA, Canada, Australia, Japan

Cover: Foto ©Paul-Georg Meister /pixelio.de

More available books at **www.hansebooks.com**

Clarendon Press Series

P. TERENTI
ADELPHI

SLOMAN

London

HENRY FROWDE

OXFORD UNIVERSITY PRESS WAREHOUSE

AMEN CORNER, E.C.

Clarendon Press Series

P. TERENTI

ADELPHI

WITH NOTES AND INTRODUCTIONS

INTENDED FOR THE HIGHER FORMS OF PUBLIC SCHOOLS

BY THE

REV. A. SLOMAN, M.A.

HEAD MASTER OF BIRKENHEAD SCHOOL
FORMERLY MASTER OF THE QUEEN'S SCHOLARS OF WESTMINSTER

Oxford
AT THE CLARENDON PRESS
1886

[All rights reserved]

PREFACE.

In the text of this edition the MSS. have been followed rather than the emendations of editors, unless there seemed to be weighty reasons to the contrary. In the absence, however, of **A**, the testimony of Donatus or other Scholiasts as to readings earlier than those in the Calliopian MSS. has been sometimes accepted, when supported by intrinsic probability. In all but a few cases the limits of space have precluded a full statement of the arguments for and against doubtful readings, but in no case has a decision been made without careful consideration of all sides of the question.

In a School edition it has been thought better to print the letter *v*, and to adopt the modernised spelling of the MSS., except in a few cases where the orthography in Terence's time was demonstrably different: e. g. *o* is substituted for *u* after another *u* or *v*; *quor, quoius, quoi, inruit*, etc., appear for *cur, cuius, cui, irruit*, etc., and *-is* for *-es* in the accusative plural of such words of the third declension as make the genitive plural in *-ium*.

It is hoped that the stage directions, which have been mainly suggested by practical experience at Westminster, may be of real service. As my opportunities of studying this aspect of the Play were unique, I have endeavoured to make this part of the edition as complete as possible.

Constant use has been made of the editions of Umpfenbach, Fleckeisen, Dziatzko, Plessis, A. Spengel, and Wagner,—the first two on textual questions only,—with less frequent reference to those of Bentley, Zeune (containing the commentaries of Donatus), Stallbaum, Parry, and Davies.

I have to thank my former fellow-worker, C. E. Freeman, Esq., of Park House School, Southborough, to whose accurate scholarship our editions of the *Trinummus* and *Andria* owed so much, for his courteous permission to make use of any matter which appeared in one of the Plays above mentioned as our joint production. I must also express my obligations to the Rev. R. F. Dale for his kindness in reading the proof-sheets and making some valuable suggestions.

A. S.

P. S.—References are made to Roby's School Latin Grammar as more likely to be generally accessible than his larger work.

BIRKENHEAD SCHOOL:
June, 1886.

CONTENTS.

INTRODUCTION: PAGE

    ROMAN COMEDY AND TERENCE . . . ix

    CHARACTERS AND PLOT OF ADELPHI . . xix

    METRES AND PROSODY OF ADELPHI . xxv

    CODICES OF TERENCE xxx

TEXT OF ADELPHI (WITH STAGE DIRECTIONS) . 1–59

LIST OF METRES OF ADELPHI 61–2

NOTES TO ADELPHI 63–121

INDEX TO NOTES 123–8

INTRODUCTION.

ROMAN COMEDY AND TERENCE.

First beginnings of Dramatic Representations at Rome. The natural bent of the Roman character was too serious and too prosaic to favour the growth of a national drama. More than five hundred years had elapsed since the foundation of the city, before a play of any kind was produced on the Roman stage, and even then it was but a rude adaptation of a foreign work by a foreign author.

Fescennine Verses. Yet there had long existed the germs whence a drama might, under other circumstances, have sprung. The unrestrained merriment of the harvest-home at time of vintage found expression, in Latium as in Greece, in extemporised dialogues more or less metrical in character, and much more than less coarse in expression. The lively genius of the Greeks had from such rude beginnings developed a regular Comedy as early as the sixth century B.C. But, among the Romans, although these rustic effusions were at a very early date sufficiently well established to receive a definite name, *Carmina Fescennina,* from Fescennia, a town in Etruria; yet they never rose above gross personalities and outrageous scurrility[1]. When this license was checked by a stringent

---

[1] See Horace Ep. 2. 1. 145 seqq.
Fescennina per hunc inventa licentia morem
Versibus alternis opprobria rustica fudit,
Libertasque recurrentes accepta per annos

clause in the Laws of the Twelve Tables, the Fescennine verses became merely a generic name for improvised songs, not always very refined, at weddings, triumphs, or other festal occasions.

Saturae. According to Livy 7. 2, the first '*ludi scenici*' were introduced at Rome 361 B.C. to appease the anger of the gods who had sent a pestilence on the city.

It seems certain that about this time a stage was erected in the Circus at the *Ludi Maximi*, and the first three days of the festival were henceforth occupied with recitations, music, and dancing. Performers from Etruria, called *ludiones*, danced to the music of the flute without words or descriptive action; but the strolling minstrels of Latium (*grassatores, spatiatores*) soon took advantage of the stage to recite their chants with appropriate music and gesture. These performances were named from their miscellaneous character **Saturae**[1]. They were composed in the rugged Saturnian metre, with no connected plot, and did not admit of dialogue.

Fabulae Atellanae. A nearer approach to dramatic form was made in the **Fabulae Atellanae**, broad farces with stock characters, e.g. Maccus, Pappus, Bucco, and Dossenus, analogous to the clown, pantaloon, and harlequin of an English pantomime. Each character had its traditional mask, and the pieces were originally played only by amateurs at private

---

Lusit amabiliter, donec iam saevus apertam
In rabiem coepit verti iocus, et per honestas
Ire domos impune minax. Doluere cruento
Dente lacessiti, fuit intactis quoque cura
Condicione super communi, quin etiam lex
Poenaque lata, malo quae nollet carmine quemquam
Describi: vertere modum formidine fustis
Ad bene dicendum delectandumque redacti.

[1] From *lanx satura*, a dish of mixed food. The later *Saturae* or Miscellanies, with which we are familiar from the works of Horace, Juvenal, and Persius, were introduced by Lucilius, who died 103 B.C. Cf. Hor. Sat. I. 10.

theatricals; but when translations from Greek dramas had monopolised the Roman stage, the Atellan farce was adopted as an after-piece, like the Satyric drama among the Greeks, and was regularly performed by professional actors. The name *Atellanae*, from Atella, an Oscan town near Capua, gave rise to the erroneous supposition that these farces were performed at Rome in the Oscan dialect; whereas it was only in accordance with Roman custom to give to dramatic performances a local name which could offend no national prejudices. The records of these plays are scanty, but they appear to have presented extravagant caricatures of special classes, trades, or occurrences, and their grotesque situations and lively humour secured them a lasting place in popular favour.

Laws regulating Dramatic Performances. The failure of the Romans to produce a national drama was due not only to their national 'gravity' but also to the rigid censorship of the laws. Any personal lampoon, any ill-advised criticism of public affairs, met with summary chastisement. *Fuste feritor* was the laconic edict of the Twelve Tables: and the magistrates seem to have had plenary power to scourge any actor at any time or place that they deemed fit.

Public opinion at Rome. To legal harshness was added a moral stigma. No Roman citizen could venture to appear on a public stage without losing his character for ever. The composition and performance of plays were handed over entirely to freedmen and slaves, who did not dare to represent Roman life, or introduce Roman topics. Even the rustic raillery and amateur farces of early Rome had to lay their scene in Tuscan Fescennia or Oscan Atella.

Contact with Greek civilisation. Moreover, in addition to a national deficiency of literary instinct, and ignominious legal penalties, a third cause had operated powerfully in checking any development of dramatic originality. For nearly five centuries the Romans had been engaged in a varying, yet almost ceaseless struggle for supremacy, or even for existence. The defeat of Pyrrhus, 274 B.C., and the final conquest of Tarentum and the other cities of Magna Graecia a few years later left them undisputed masters of the whole peninsula. They were thus brought into close contact with Greek civilisation at the very moment when they had leisure to attend to it. There began at once to arise an ever-increasing demand for a better education for the Roman youth, and for more varied amusements for the Roman populace. The satisfaction of these demands was delayed by the First Punic War, 264-241 B.C.

Livius Andronicus. In the next year Livius Andronicus, a Tarentine captive who received his freedom for educating the sons of Livius Salinator, produced on the Roman stage[1] a drama translated from the Greek. He also translated the Odyssey into Saturnian verse as an educational text-book, which was still in use in the boyhood of Horace[2]. Thus at Rome the beginnings both of Epic and Dramatic poetry were due not so much to poetical inspiration as to the needs of the school-room and the Circus. As might be expected in work thus done to order, there was little artistic merit. The few fragments which remain seem crude and barbarous, and we may well believe that the books were never again opened when the rod of an Orbilius was no longer dreaded.

Old Athenian Comedy. There could be no doubt as to the school of Attic Comedy to be chosen for imitation. The Old Comedy of Eupolis, Cratinus or Aristophanes, essentially political in its subjects, abounding in topical allusions and trenchant

---

[1] *Serus enim Graecis admovit acumina chartis,*
Et post Punica bella quietus quaerere coepit,
Quid Sophocles et Thespis et Aeschylus utile ferrent.
                              Hor. Ep. 2. 1. 161-163.

[2] *Non equidem insector delendave carmina Livi*
Esse reor, memini quae plagosum mihi parvo
Orbilium dictare.
                              Hor. Ep. 1. 2. 1. 69-71.

satire of public men and public matters, could not have been reproduced on a Roman stage.

Middle Comedy. Even the poets of the Middle Comedy, who satirised classes rather than individuals or travestied schools of philosophy, would have seemed far too free to the stern censors of the Republic, and would have been almost unintelligible to the majority of Romans.

New Comedy. The New Comedy was alone available. This was the name given to a school of dramatists, of whom the best known are Philemon, Diphilus, Apollodorus of Carystus, and above all Menander. They wrote at a period (340-260 B.C.) when the power of Macedon had crushed the liberty of Greece. Political life was dead; social life was idle and corrupt. The natural products of such a period of decay were the 'Society' plays of the New Comedy. Their aim was merely to give amusing sketches of every-day life[1]. The savage satire of Aristophanes only survived in good-humoured banter. The keen strife of Conservatism against Democracy was replaced by intrigues of amorous youths or crafty slaves to out-wit the head of the family. The interest of these plays was not local but cosmopolitan. Human nature is pretty much the same in all ages, and so these plays were naturally suited for the Roman stage. They were amusing, without the slightest tendency to criticise points of national interest, or otherwise offend against the strict regulations of the Roman magistrates.

Cn. Naevius, 235-204 B.C., the first imitator of Livius Andronicus, a Campanian of great ability and force of character, did indeed dare to write with something of Aristophanic freedom. But his temerity in assailing the haughty Metelli, and even the mighty Africanus himself, led first to imprisonment and afterwards to banishment. The experiment was not repeated.

---

[1] Cf. Cic. Rep. 4. 11 *imitationem vitae, speculum consuetudinis, imaginem veritatis.*

Plautus and Terence. Between 230 and 160 B.C. the writers of Comedy were fairly numerous[1], but only two have bequeathed to posterity more than scattered fragments. These two are Titus Maccius Plautus and Publius Terentius Afer.

Life and Works of Terence. Plautus died in 184 B.C. Terence was born in 195 B.C. at Carthage, whence his cognomen 'Afer.' He was a slave, but must early have shown signs of ability, for his master, Terentius Lucanus, gave him a good education, and before long his freedom. His talents gained him admission to the literary clique, known as the Scipionic circle, the fashionable representatives of the new Hellenic culture. Scipio Aemilianus was the centre of the coterie, which included Laelius and Furius Philo, Sulpicius Gallus, Q. Fabius Labeo, M. Popillius, the philosopher Panaetius, and the historian Polybius. These being men of education and taste, unreservedly recognised the immeasurable superiority of Greek literature as compared with the rude efforts of their native writers. To present to a Roman audience a faithful reproduction of the best Hellenic models, in pure and polished Latin, seemed to them the ideal of literary excellence. Style was more valued than strength, correctness of form more than originality of thought. Such was the literary atmosphere which Terence breathed; and his enemies, not confining themselves to gross aspersions on his moral character, openly affirmed that the plays produced under his name were really the work of his distinguished patrons. How far Scipio or Laelius may have had some hand in his plays can never be known; Terence at any rate did not care to refute the report which doubtless flattered his noble friends, but rather prided himself on the intimacy and approbation of so select a circle[2]. All the plays of Terence, as

---

[1] e.g. Caecilius, Licinius, Atilius, and others. Ennius, whose fame rests on his Epic poem, also adapted Greek plays, chiefly tragedies, to the Roman stage.

[2] *Nam quod isti dicunt malevoli, homines nobilis*
   Eum adiutare adsidueque una scribere;

of Plautus, were *Comoediae palliatae*, i.e. plays wherein the scene and characters are Greek, as opposed to *Comoediae togatae*, where the scene is laid in Rome or at least in Italy. *Praetextatae* was a name given to historic or tragic plays.

Terence's first comedy, the Andria, was produced 166 B.C. Suetonius relates that when this play was offered to the Aediles, the young author was told to submit it to the judgment of Caecilius. Terence arrived when the veteran poet was at supper, and being in mean attire was seated on a stool near the table. But he had read no more than a few lines, when Caecilius bade him take a place upon his couch, and bestowed high commendation on the play. As Caecilius died in 168 B.C., the Andria must have been in manuscript at least two years before its performance, and some colour is given to the above anecdote by the mention which Terence makes in the Prologue of the ill-natured criticisms of Luscius Lanuvinus. The Hecyra, his second play, proved his least successful one. At its first performance in 165 B.C., the audience deserted the theatre to look at some boxers; a similar fate attended a second representation in 160 B.C., and only the personal intercession of the manager, Ambivius Turpio, secured it a hearing at all. The Hauton Timorumenos appeared in 163, the Eunuchus and Phormio in 161, the Adelphi in 160. In the same year Terence visited Greece, either to study for himself Athenian manners and customs, or, as some assert, to escape the persecution of his enemies. According to one account[1] he perished by shipwreck in 159 B.C., as he was returning to Italy with no less than 108 of Menander's comedies translated into Latin. A more general

---

Quod illi maledictum vehemens esse existumant,
Eam laudem hic ducit maximam, quom illis placet,
Qui vobis univorsis et populo placent,
Quorum opera in bello, in otio, in negotio
Suo quisque tempore ususd sine superbia.

Adelphi Prol. 15-21.

[1] Cf. Suetonius, Vita Terenti 4-5.

belief was that he died at Stymphalus, in Arcadia, from grief on hearing of the loss of his MSS., which he had sent on before him by sea. Porcius Licinus narrates that his noble patrons suffered him to die in such abject poverty that he had not even a lodging at Rome whither a slave might have brought news of his death. This is probably untrue, for Suetonius writes that he left gardens of twenty jugera in extent on the Appian Way, and his daughter afterwards married a Roman knight.

In personal appearance Terence is said to have been of middle height, with a slight figure and reddish-brown hair. Of his character we know nothing, save what can be gathered from his prologues. These indicate a lack of independence and confidence. He evidently feels that he is not a popular poet. He never professes to be more than an adapter from Greek models; imitation, not creation, was the object of his art.

Contrast of Plautus and Terence. This sensitive *protégé* of patrician patrons has none of the vigorous personality of Plautus. Indeed, though the literary activity of the two poets is only separated by a single generation, their works belong to different epochs of literature. Plautus wrote for the people, he aimed at the broad effect on the stage, his fun was natural and not unfrequently boisterous. Circumstances forced him to adapt foreign plays and lay his scenes in foreign cities, but he was not careful to disguise his true nationality, and freely introduced Roman names, allusions, and customs wherever they might contribute to the dramatic effect on the heterogeneous audience which crowded to the gratuitous entertainments of a Roman holiday.

Between such plays and the polished productions of Terence there is a world of difference. Terence sought the approbation, not of the uncultured masses, but of a select circle of literary men. His highest aim was to produce in the purest Latin a perfect representation of the comedies of Menander and his school. His cardinal virtues, as a writer, were correctness of language and consistency of character. His scene is always laid at Athens, and not once in his six plays is to be found an allusion which is distinctively Roman. Indeed, the whole tone of his writings was cosmopolitan. Human nature, under the somewhat common-place conditions of every-day life in a civilised community, was his subject; *Homo sum, humani nihil a me alienum puto*, was his motto. His plays breathe a spirit of broad-minded liberality, and their simple unaffected style, the easy yet pointed dialogue, the terse and dramatic descriptions, and the admirable delicacy of the portrayal of character, won for Terence from the cultured taste of the Augustan age a more favourable verdict[1] than he could have expected from the rude and unlettered masses who most enjoyed the broad fun of a boisterous farce. The above characteristics secured for Terence considerable attention at the Renaissance in Europe. In England several of the minor dramatists are under obligations to him; while in France his influence profoundly affected Molière, and is in no small degree responsible for the long-continued servitude of the French drama to the 'unities' of time and place which have so cramped its free development.

As might be expected, the characters in Terence, though admirably drawn, are rather commonplace. No personality in his plays stands out in the memory like that of Tyndarus in the *Captivi*, or Stasimus in the *Trinummus*. Two old men, one irascible and the other mild, both usually the dupes of their

---

[1] Afranius writes:
Terentio non similem dices quempiam.
Cicero writes:
Tu quoque, qui solus lecto sermone, Terenti,
Conversum expressumque Latina voce Menandrum
In medium nobis sedatis vocibus effers,
Quidquid come loquens atque omnia dulcia dicens.
Horace, Ep. 2. 1. 59, records the general verdict:
dicitur ...
Vincere Caecilius gravitate, Terentius arte.
Volcatius, on the other hand, places Terence below Naevius, Plautus, Caecilius, Licinius, and Atilius.

sons and an intriguing slave; two young men, one of strong character and the other weak, both amorous and somewhat unscrupulous as to the means of gratifying their passion; a dignified and elderly gentleman; an anxious mother; a devoted servant; a rascally slave dealer: these form the stock characters of Terentian comedy and recur with somewhat wearisome monotony. Nor does the standard of morality rise above a conventional respectability and a civilised consideration for others, except where the natural impulses inspire a generous disposition with something of nobility.

The discerning criticism of Caesar nearly expresses the more matured judgment of modern times:

> *Tu quoque, tu in summis, O dimidiate Menander,*
> *Poneris et merito, puri sermonis amator.*
> *Lenibus atque utinam scriptis adiuncta foret vis*
> *Comica, ut aequato virtus polleret honore*
> *Cum Graecis neque in hac despectus parte iaceres;*
> *Unum hoc maceror ac doleo tibi deesse, Terenti.*

Not that Terence was devoid of humour; but his humour is so delicate and refined that it must often have fallen flat upon the stage. When his plays are well known their subtle satire and polished wit can be appreciated; but there is without doubt an absence of energy and action (Caesar's *vis comica*), which prevented his pieces from being dramatically successful. An audience must be educated up to his plays before it can perceive their many excellences.

THE EXTANT COMEDIES OF TERENCE.

Andria.
Hecyra.
Hauton Timorumenos.
Eunuchus.
Phormio.
Adelphi.

THE CHARACTERS AND PLOT OF THE ADELPHI.

The Adelphi derives its title from the contrasted types of character presented to us in the two brothers Micio and Demea, and in a lesser degree in Demea's two sons Aeschinus and Ctesipho.

But the interest of the Adelphi is not confined to a skilful delineation of character, much less to a lively plot or farcical situations.

The author had a deeper purpose in view than the mere amusement of a Roman crowd. He had thought much on the subject of education, and this play cannot be fully understood unless we perceive the underlying principle which the whole development of the piece is intended to illustrate. So consummate is the artistic skill of the poet that the moral is never obtruded upon our notice; indeed, a superficial reader may know the comedy well without ever suspecting that there is a moral at all, though many such readers have been rather puzzled by the apparent change of Demea's character in Act V.

Terence takes two opposite theories of education of which Micio and Demea are respectively the representatives.

Micio was an easy-going city bachelor who had adopted Aeschinus, the elder of his brother Demea's two sons. He liked to enjoy life in his own way, and was willing to allow other people a similar license. In accordance with these principles he gave to Aeschinus the fullest liberty of action. The young man was free to do what he liked, go where he pleased, and draw money without stint. Micio disbelieved in education by fear, and thought that by such means he would gain the confidence and love of his adopted son; and that even if Aeschinus did sow his wild oats somewhat recklessly no permanent harm would be done. The result sadly disappointed his expectations. He had endeavoured to inculcate one thing above all others, that Aeschinus should be perfectly frank and open, concealing nothing and disguising nothing (52-8). Yet Micio first hears of the abduction of the music-girl from Demea, when all the town was already talking of it (93). And still worse, for nine months Aeschinus had been paying daily visits to Pamphila in the very next house (293), carefully keeping Micio in ignorance of the whole affair (640); nor does his honour, on which his uncle placed such reliance, prevent him from telling a direct lie (641) under fear of discovery. Micio's theory, therefore, of unlimited indulgence proves a complete failure: the opposite system of strict repression we shall find equally unsuccessful.

Demea is an old-fashioned country gentleman, thrifty in his manner of life, violent in temper, uncompromising in opinion. He has brought up his younger son, Ctesipho, under the most rigid discipline. He flatters himself that nothing goes on without his knowledge (396, 546-8), and that his son is a really steady young man, who is entirely innocent of his brother's wicked ways (94-6). Yet, in spite of all this careful training and supervision, Ctesipho becomes deeply involved in an intrigue with a music-girl, while Demea is still living in his fool's paradise.

These events open Demea's eyes to the truth. He sees that his own extreme strictness and Micio's over-indulgence have been alike mistaken. In Act V he demonstrates the shallowness of Micio's views by a delightfully humorous *reductio ad absurdum*, and finally in a few serious words (985-995) indicates that in liberty duly restrained by a father's advice and correction lies the golden mean of a young man's education.

With regard to the minor characters few words will suffice. Unfettered freedom has made Aeschinus reckless and overbearing towards inferiors (e.g. 182, 198-9), and the absence of any moral training renders him ready to yield to temptations of deceit and falsehood. Ctesipho, on the other hand, is timid and desponding. He depends on Aeschinus to obtain the object of his love, and on Syrus to keep her. Still both the youths are naturally of good disposition, however much they may have been perverted by training and circumstance. The elder is generous to a fault, affectionate towards his brother and adopted uncle, faithful to his young wife, and ready to confess his failings when presented to him in their true light. The younger is simple and unaffected, almost extravagantly grateful to Aeschinus, shocked at the mere suggestion of a lie, though too weak to resist the bad influence of a stronger character.

The action of the play is largely carried on, as is usual in comedies of this class, by a confidential slave. Syrus is a clever and unscrupulous rogue, who encourages the young men in their dissipation, and whose character is only made tolerable by the exquisite irony with which he banters Demea. In strong contrast is the honest and impetuous Geta, and the faithful Canthara, both servants of Sostrata.

Hegio is a gentleman of the old school, poor indeed, but dignified, and of unswerving fidelity towards the widow of his old friend ; while Sostrata excites our real sympathy by her devoted affection and courageous honesty of purpose.

Sannio, the slave-dealer, is mercenary and repulsive. His

low-bred bluster in Act II forms an admirable foil to the quiet decision and contemptuous sarcasm of the gentleman.

Before the action of the play begins both the young men had fallen in love. Aeschinus indeed had been for nine months secretly married to Pamphila, daughter of Sostrata, while Ctesipho had formed an apparently hopeless attachment to a music-girl who was a slave of Sannio. A son of Demea could not be expected to have sufficient ready money to buy an expensive slave; but Aeschinus, hearing of his brother's despair, boldly broke into the house and carried off the girl in spite of her owner's resistance.

Act I. It is just after this event that the curtain rises on Micio, who, finding that Aeschinus has been absent from home all night, proceeds to dilate on the anxieties of parents and the best method of education. He is interrupted (Sc. 2) by Demea, who has heard of his elder son's escapade, and fiercely assails Micio for encouraging conduct so scandalous. The city-bred brother is, however, more than a match in argument for his rustic opponent, who is silenced, though not convinced.

Act II. Aeschinus now appears leading the music-girl, followed by Sannio, who endeavours to prevent her from entering Micio's house, but only gets soundly cuffed for his pains. In the next scene (Sc. 2), Syrus is sent out to bring Sannio to terms, and so works on the fears of the dealer that he would gladly accept the cost-price of the girl, if only he could be sure of that. Syrus is saved from the necessity of making rash promises by the appearance of Ctesipho (Sc. 3), overjoyed at the exploit of his brother, whom he presently (Sc. 4) meets and thanks most affectionately.

Act III introduces us to Sostrata, who is expressing her anxiety to Canthara, her nurse, when Geta (Sc. 2) appears, violently agitated at the apparent unfaithfulness of Aeschinus towards Pamphila. Sostrata resolves to appeal to Hegio, an old friend of the family. Demea now reappears (Sc. 3), furious at the news that Ctesipho is implicated in the abduction of the music-girl. By adroit lies Syrus turns all the facts to Ctesipho's credit, and in a scene of delicious humour first draws out and then parodies the old man's foibles. Demea is about to seek his son when (Sc. 4) Geta brings up Hegio, who narrates the supposed desertion of Pamphila by Aeschinus and declares his intention of strenuously defending Sostrata and her daughter. Demea departs to pour out the vials of his wrath on Micio.

In **Act IV. Scene 1**, Ctesipho and Syrus are all but surprised together by Demea, who returns from a fruitless search after his brother, having been told by a labourer that his errant son had not been seen at the country-house. Syrus however (Sc. 2) is equal to the occasion, and covering one lie by another sends off Demea on a wild-goose chase after Micio, while he himself retires to kill time with just a glass or two.

In the next scene (Sc. 3) Micio and Hegio come on conversing. In place of denials or evasions Hegio receives assurances of most ample satisfaction, and Micio at once visits Sostrata to allay her anxiety.

Scene 4 shows us Aeschinus, much distressed at the suspicions which have fallen upon him, yet unwilling to expose his brother. He is about to enter Sostrata's house when confronted by Micio (Sc. 5), who, as a punishment for his want of confidence, torments him with a feigned story about Pamphila's intended marriage with another man. Aeschinus, unable to keep on the mask longer, bursts into tears, whereupon Micio, after an affectionate reproof, promises to acknowledge Pamphila as his wife.

(Sc. 6) Demea returns from his vain peregrination, angry and foot-sore. Already boiling with indignation he is goaded almost to madness (Sc. 7) by his brother's cool indifference to all that is most outrageous, and in this humour is found by Syrus, who enters intoxicated (Sc. 8). His drunken insolence is interrupted by a message from Ctesipho, who is within. Demea forces his way into the house (Sc. 9), whence he bursts out upon Micio with furious invective, though, as before, he is eventually reduced by his brother's readier tongue to an unwilling acquiescence.

Act V. Experience, though late, has taught Demea that his system of education is as unsuccessful as his brother's, while his churlish and parsimonious habits gain him nothing but enemies. He resolves therefore to correct his own mistakes, and to teach Micio how far he has erred in the opposite extreme. The monologue in Scene 1 is spoken in the fictitious character which he is about to play in furtherance of this object. He at once proceeds to outbid Micio in courtesy and complaisance. He flatters Syrus (Sc. 2), and Geta (Sc. 3); he orders (Sc. 4) the marriage of Aeschinus to be ratified immediately, and the partition wall between the gardens of Micio and Sostrata to be pulled down. With the aid of Aeschinus (Sc. 5) he forces from the astonished Micio a reluctant consent to marry Sostrata, to present Hegio with a farm, and to set free Syrus with his wife: he even sanctions the marriage of Ctesipho with the music-girl. He is naturally greeted with a chorus of effusive flattery; whereupon, dropping the part which he had been playing, he shows Micio how cheap is the popularity gained by indiscriminate indulgence, and closes the play with some sensible advice to the young men.

The verdict of posterity on the Adelphi is shown by the number of modern plays wholly or partly based upon it. Garrick's *Guardian*, Baron's *École des Pères*, and Fagan's *La pupille* are direct adaptations.

Micio and Demea are the originals of leading characters in Cumberland's *Choleric Man*, Shadwell's *Squire of Alsatia*, and Diderot's *La Père de famille*, and the greatest of French Comedians is under no inconsiderable obligations to the same source in his *École des Maris*.

On the stage the Andria may be equally effective, but from a literary point of view the Adelphi is beyond question the masterpiece of Terence.

METRES AND PROSODY.

The object of this Introduction is to explain briefly the metres employed by Terence in the Adelphi, and to clear up such apparent difficulties of Prosody as may remain after the general scheme of the metres is understood.

These metres (with the exception of a Choriambic line 613) are Iambic and Trochaic, which receive their names from being composed of iambi or trochees, as the case may be, or of some other feet, considered to be equivalent: and the lines are further subdivided according to the number of metres which they contain, and according to their complete or incomplete form. In iambic and trochaic lines a series of two feet is called a *metre* (or dipodia), and the name of the line corresponds to the number of these metres; thus an iambic trimeter is an iambic line, containing three metres or six feet; a trochaic tetrameter is a trochaic line, containing four metres or eight feet. Again, some lines have a number of complete feet; these are called acatalectic; while others are called catalectic, because the last foot is incomplete. Thus a trochaic tetrameter catalectic is a trochaic line of four metres or eight feet, wanting the last syllable, and really containing only seven feet and a half.

I. IAMBIC.

(*a*) **Iambic Trimeter Acatalectic, or Senarius**: (578[1]); all the plays of Terence begin with it.

(*b*) **Iambic Tetrameter Acatalectic**, called **Octonarius**, from its eight complete feet. (186.)

(*c*) **Iambic Tetrameter Catalectic**, called **Septenarius**, from its seven complete feet. (6.)

---

[1] These figures, here and below, indicate the number of lines of the metre in question in this Play.

(*d*) **Iambic Dimeter Acatalectic, or Quaternarius.** (3.)

(*e*) **Iambic Dimeter Catalectic.** (1 ; in 612 b.)

These lines consist in their pure form of iambi; but the spondee, tribrach, anapaest, and dactyl are admitted in all feet except the last, which must be an iambus, unless, of course, the verse is catalectic. Moreover, as the Tetrameter is regarded as being composed of two verses, with the division after the fourth foot, that foot is usually an iambus; and such words as *ego*, *tibi*, *cedo*, are allowed to stand there as if at the end of a senarius.

II. TROCHAIC.

(*a*) **Trochaic Tetrameter Acatalectic, or Octonarius.** (18.)

(*b*) **Trochaic Tetrameter Catalectic, or Septenarius.** (201.)

(*c*) **Trochaic Dimeter Catalectic.** (4.)

These lines consist in their pure form of trochees; the spondee, tribrach, anapaest, and dactyl are also admitted. But only the trochee, tribrach, and sometimes dactyl are found in the seventh foot of the Septenarius; and the eighth foot of the Octonarius is always a trochee or spondee. Trochaic, like Iambic Tetrameters, are considered to be divided after the fourth foot. As the Trochaic metre is more quick and lively than the Iambic, it is naturally employed in scenes where feeling and excitement are represented. In any of the metres above mentioned the spondee is occasionally resolved into a Proceleusmatic ($\smile\smile\smile\smile$), which is most commonly in the first foot and composed of two distinct pairs of syllables. Cf. 35, 118, 192, 254, 264, 523, 845, 900, 938.

Besides the above, 613 seems to be Choriambic, composed of 3 choriambi ($-\smile\smile-$); and 610 *a* is an irregular line, apparently made up of one iambic dipodia with a syllable over. But the metres in the short *Canticum* 610–7 are very uncertain.

Prosody. The rules of prosody, as commonly taught, must be considerably modified, if we are to understand the scansion of Plautus and Terence. It must always be remembered that the poets of the late days of the Republic and their successors were writing in a literary language, not in the language of every-day life. The quantity of any syllable was regarded as rigidly fixed, just as we might find it marked in a dictionary. But in reading the comic poets we find that *accent* must be considered as well as quantity. Scansion was determined by the ear, not by any hard and fast rules. Just as in Shakesperian verse *loved* may be scanned as of one syllable or of two, and the same word may be pronounced as long or short according to its position, so in Terence *eius, huius, quoius,* etc., may be monosyllabic or dissyllabic, and the same syllable may be used with a different quantity according to the requirements of the metre. This latter variation of quantity is however not arbitrary, but conforms to a general law, which may be thus stated.

When the metrical accent falls on the first syllable of an Iambus, or on the syllable before or after an Iambus, the second syllable of the Iambus may be shortened.

Accordingly in Iambic metre,

(a) $-\acute{\smile}- = -\acute{\smile}\smile$, (b) $\smile-\acute{-} = \smile\smile\acute{-}$:

in Trochaic metre,

(c) $\acute{-}\smile- = \acute{-}\smile\smile$,

(d) $\acute{\smile}-- = \acute{\smile}\smile-$, (e) $\acute{\smile}-\smile = \acute{\smile}\smile\smile$.

It will be noted that in the following examples some of the shortened syllables would by the ordinary rules be long by nature, others long by position.

(a) 239 *labáscit. únum hŏc hábeo : vĭdĕ si sătĭs placét.*

605 *omnés, quibŭs rés sunt mĭnŭs secúndae, mágĭs sunt, néscio quó modó.*

(b) 73 *studĕt păr refĕrre.*

638 *quid huĭc hĭc negŏti est.*

900 *studĕnt făcere* (in a proceleusmatic).

This form of shortening, i.e. where the metrical accent falls on the syllable *after* the iambus, is by far the most frequent.

(c) 167 *ăbĭ prae strĕ́nue ăc forĭs ăperi.*
   517 *dĭ́c sodĕ́s. apŭ́d vĭllam est.* Cf. 680.
(d) 198 *dŏ́mŏ me erĭ́puit.*
   525 *prĭŭs nox ŏppressĭ́sset.* Cf. 167 in (c.)
(e) 544 *quĭd hŏ́c, malum, ĭnfelĭ́citatis.*
   699 *ăbĭ domum ăc deos cŏ́mprecăre.*

Some scholars maintain that Latin pronunciation threw the accent on the first syllable, so that in the case of an iambus the stress laid upon the short syllable tended to shorten the long syllable; and in support of their theory they cite the quantities of *mălĕ, quăsĭ, cĭtŏ* as contrasted with *cērtē, ētsī, rārō*, etc. Others consider that the *metrical* accent is alone sufficient to account for all shortened syllables. The true explanation will probably be found in a combination of both theories, i.e. that a natural tendency of colloquial pronunciation to shorten the long syllable of an iambus was extended by the incidence of the metrical accent. At any rate the law seems clearly established, though its origin may be doubtful.

But besides the law above mentioned, there are other causes of difference between Terentian and Augustan prosody.

I. Indifference to double consonants, which Terence probably did not write. Thus *ille* is often used as a pyrrhic (⌣ ⌣), e.g. 72, 211, etc., so too 238 *ŏppressionem*, 603 *ŏfficio*, 720 *ĕccum*.

II. Retention of the quantity of final syllables originally long. This is much less common in Terence than in Plautus, and many instances given by Wagner are doubtful. Probably this retention only takes place when helped by the *arsis*, and usually at a pause. Cf. 25 *augeāt iudustriam*, 27 *īerant*.

III. Synizesis. Almost any two vowels not separated by a consonant may be contracted into a single syllable. This is most common in the case of pronouns, e.g. 10 $\overline{eum}$, 114 $\overline{tuom}$, 160 $\overline{meorum}$, 581 $\overline{huius}$, 648 $\overline{eas}$; also in other words, e.g. 79 *nescīō*, 160 *fuīsse*, 225 $\overline{coe}$*misse*, 573 $\overline{deo}$*rsum*, 971 $\overline{seo}$*rsum*, etc. Sometimes a word made monosyllabic by synizesis is then elided, e.g. 10 *ēŭm*, 854 *rēī*. In Terence *dehinc* and *proin* are always of one syllable, and *antehac* of two. Note, however, that *nunc iam* is always scanned *nūncĭăm*, and is printed accordingly.

IV. **Hiatus** is admitted,

(1) When there is a change of speaker, e.g. 604, 697, 767.

(2) When the line is broken by a strong pause, e.g. 574.

(3) After an interjection, e.g. 183, 304, 336. Note, however, that *O may* be elided, e.g. 407, 449.

Occasionally a long final vowel, or a vowel before *m* is shortened and not elided, e. g. 111 *mĕ ad*, 118 *dŭm erit*, 215 *quĭ hodie*, and in lines 232, 336, 341, 527, 618, 680, 705, 920. Cf. Verg. Ecl. 8. 108 *an quĭ amant*.

CODICES OF TERENCE.

The MSS. of Terence fall into two classes. Class I is before the recension of Calliopius, Class II after it. Class II is arranged in probable order of antiquity.

CLASS I.

Letter of Reference.	Name of Codex.	Place where it is now kept.	Century.	Remarks.
A.	BEMBINUS.	Vatican.	IV or V.	On parchment in uncial characters.

CLASS II.

Letter of Reference.	Name of Codex.	Place where it is now kept.	Century.	Remarks.
D.	VICTORIANUS.	Vatican.	IX or X.	Also known as C. Laurentianus.
P.	PARISINUS.	Paris.	IX or X.	On parchment in small characters.
C.	VATICANUS.	Vatican.	IX or X.	Copied by a German from the same original as P.
F.	AMBROSIANUS.	Milan.	IX or X.	Andria wanting.
B.	BASILICANUS.	Vatican.	X.	A copy of C., except a gap which was filled up from D.
V.	FRAGMENTUM VINDOBONENSE.	Vienna.	X or XI.	Six sheets containing Andria 912–981.
E.	RICCARDIANUS.	Florence.	XI.	Andria 1–39 wanting.
G.	DECURTATUS.	Vatican.	XI or XII.	Much mutilated.

The Bembine is by far the most important, not merely on account of its antiquity, but because it alone has escaped the recension of Calliopius in the seventh century. Codex A was in bad condition, as its owner Cardinal Bembo testified before the end of the fifteenth century. Andria 1–786 is now entirely wanting, and of Adelphi 914–997 only a few letters are legible.

It bears a note written by Politian (1493 A.D.) to the effect that he never saw so old a Codex. The hands of two correctors can be discerned: one of ancient date, which only appears twice in the Andria, and never in the Phormio or Adelphi; the other about the fifteenth century, which changed and added characters in a 'downright shameless fashion.' But, where not thus tampered with, Codex A possesses an authority sufficient to outweigh all the other MSS. taken together. The later MSS. were so much altered by the Calliopian recension that their independent authority is not very great. In all MSS., even in A, the spelling has been much modernised.

The evidence of the MSS. is to some small extent supplemented by quotations of ancient writers and the commentaries of grammarians.

Of these latter, the most important is Aelius Donatus, tutor of St. Jerome, about 350 A. D., and author of a celebrated grammatical treatise which became the common text-book of mediaeval schools. Priscian (480 ? A.D.), Servius (about 420 A.D.) in his notes on Vergil, and other more obscure scholiasts are of occasional service.

P. TERENTI
ADELPHI.

INCIPIT · TERENTI · ADELPHOE ·
GRAECA · MENANDRV ·
ACTA · LVDIS · FVNERALIB · L · AEMILIO · PAVLO ·
QVOS · FECERE ·
Q · FABIVS · MAXIMVS · P · CORNELIVS · AFRICANVS ·
EGERE ·
L · ATILIVS · PRAENESTINVS · L · AMBIVIVS · TVRPIO ·
MODOS · FECIT ·
FLACCVS · CLAVDI · TIBIIS · SARRANIS · TOTA ·
FACTA · VI ·
M · CORNELIO · CETHEGO · L · ANICIO · GALLO · COS ·

PERSONAE.

MICIO SENEX
DEMEA SENEX
SANNIO MERCATOR
AESCHINVS ADVLESCENS
SYRVS SERVOS
CTESIPHO ADVLESCENS
SOSTRATA MATRONA
CANTHARA NVTRIX
GETA SERVOS
HEGIO SENEX
DROMO SERVOS.

PERSONAE MVTAE.

PARMENO SERVOS
PSALTRIA.

ADELPHI.

PROLOGVS.

Postquám poëta sénsit scripturám suam
Ab iníquis observári et advorsários
Rapere ín peiorem pártem quam acturí sumus:
Indício de se ipse érit, vos eritis iúdices,
Laudín an vitio dúci id factum opórteat.   5
Synápothnescontes Díphili comoédia est:
Eam Cómmorientis Plaútus fecit fábulam.
In Graéca adulescens ést, qui domino eius éripit
Ancíllam in prima fábula: eum Plautús locum
Relíquit integrum. eum híc locum sumpsít sibi   10
In Adélphos, verbum dé verbo expressum éxtulit.
Eam nós acturi súmŭs novam: pernőscite
Furtúmne factum exístumetis án locum
Reprehénsum, qui praetéritus neglegéntia est.
Nam quód isti dicunt málevoli, homines nóbilis   15
Eum ádiutare adsídueque una scríbere:
Quod illí maledictum vehémens esse exístumant,
Eam laúdem hic ducit máxumam, quom illís placet,
Qui vóbis univórsis et populó placent,
Quorum ópera in bello, in ótio, in negótio   20
Suo quísque tempore úsust sine supérbia.
Dehinc ne éxpectetis árgumentum fábulae:
Senés qui primi vénient, ii partem áperient,
In agéndo partem osténdent. facite aequánimitas
Poétae ad scribendum aúgeāt indústriam.   25

ACTVS I.

SC. 1.

MICIO.

(*Athens: a place where four streets meet. The houses of Micio and Sostrata open on the stage. The scene is unchanged throughout the play.*

Enter Micio from his house. He calls through the door for Storax, then, after waiting in vain for an answer, advances to the front of the stage.)

Storáx!—non rediit hác nocte a cena Aéschinus,
Neque sérvolorum quísquam, qui advorsum ferant.
Profécto hoc vere dícunt: si absis úspiam,
Aut íbi si cesses, évenire ea sátius est
Quae in te úxor dicit ét quae in animo cógitat   5 30
Iráta, quam illa quaé parentes própitii.
Vxór, si cesses, aút te amare cógitat
Aut téte amari aut pótare atque animo óbsequi,
[Et tíbi bene esse, sóli quom sibi sít male.]
Ego, quía non rediit fílius, quae cógito!   10 35
Quibŭs núnc sollicitor rébus! ne aut ille álserit
Aut úspiam ecíderit, aut praefrégerit
Aliquíd. Vah! quemquamne hóminem in animum in-
  stítuere
Paráre quod sit cárius quam ipse ést sibi!
Atque éx me hic natus nón est, sed ĕx fratre. Ís adeo 15 40
Dissímili studio est iam índe ab adulescéntia.

Ego hánc clementem vítam urbanam atque ótium
Secútus sum et, quod fórtunatum istí putant,
Vxórem numquam habui. ílle contra haec ómnia
Ruri ágere vitam: sémper parce ac dúriter   20   45
Se habére: uxorem dúxit: nati fílii
Duo: índe ego hunc maiórem adoptaví mihi:
Edúxi a parvolo, hábui, amavi pró meo;
In eó me oblecto: sólum id est carúm mihi.
Ille út item contra me hábeat, facio sédulo.   25   50
Do, praétermitto: nón necesse habeo ómnia
Pro meó iure agere: póstremo, alii clánculum
Patrés quae faciunt, quaé fert adulescéntia,
Ea né me celet, cónsuefeci fílium.
Nam quí mentiri aut fállere insuerít patrem,   30   55
Fraudáre tanto mágis audebit céteros.
Pudóre et liberálitate líberos
Retinére satius ésse credo quám metu.
Haec frátri mecum nón conveniunt néque placent.
Venit ád me saepe clámans, 'quid agis, Mício?   35   60
Quor pérdis adulescéntem nobis? quór amat?
Quor pótat? quor tu his rébus sumptum súggeris?
Vestítu nimio indúlges: nimiùm inéptus es.'
Nimium ípse est durus praéter aequomque ét bonum:
Et érrat longe meá quidem senténtia,   40   65
Qui inpérium credat grávius esse aut stábilius,
Vi quód fit, quam illud quód amicitia adiúngitur.
Mea síc est ratio et síc animum inducó meum:
Maló coactus quí suom officiúm facit,
Dum id réscitum iri crédit, tantispér pavet: 45   70
Si spérat fore clam, rúrsum ad ingeniúm redit.
Ille quém beneficio adiúngas, ex animó facit,
Studět pár referre, praésens absensque ídem erit.

Hoc pátrium est, potius cónsuefacere fílium
Sua spónte recte fácere quam alienó metu: 50 75
Hoc páter ac dominus ínterest: hoc quí nequit,
Fateátur nescire ínperare líberis. (*turns to go off, when he catches sight of Demea coming towards him.*)
Sed éstne hic ipse, dé quo agebam? et cérte is est.
Nescío quid tristem vídeo: credo iam, út solet,
Iurgábit, (*enter Demea in manifest ill-humour. Micio advances cordially with outstretched hand.*) salvom te ádvenire, Démea, 55 80
Gaudémus.

SC. 2.

DEMEA. MICIO.

DE. (*bluntly ignoring Micio's proffered salutation.*) Ehem opportúne! te ipsum quaérito.
MI. Quid trístis es? **DE.** (*angrily.*) Rogás me, ubi nobis Aéschinus
Siét, quid tristis égo sim? **MI.** (*aside.*) Dixin hóc fore?
(*alóud.*) Quid fécit? **DE.** (*with a passionate outburst.*) Quid ílle fécerit? quem néque pudet
Quicquám, nec metuit quémquam, neque legém putat 5 85
Tenére se ullam: nam ílla quae antehac fácta sunt
Omítto: modo quid désignavit? **MI.** Quídnam id est?
DE. Forís effregit, átque in aedis ínruit
Aliénas: ipsum dóminum atque omnem fámiliam
Mulcávit usque ad mórtem: eripuit múlierem 10 90
Quam amábat. clamant ómnes indigníssume
Factum ésse: hoc adveniénti quot mihi, Mícío,
Dixére! in ore est ómni populo. dénique,
Si cónferendum exémplum est, non fratrém videt

Rei dáre operam, ruri ésse parcum ac sóbrium? 15 95
Nullum húius simile fáctum. haec quom illi, Mício,
Dicó, tibi dico: tu íllum corrumpí sinis.
MI. *(quietly.)* Homine ínperito númquam quicquam in-
    iústius,
Qui nísi quod ipse fécit nil rectúm putat.
DE. Quorsum ístuc? MI. Quia tu, Démea, haec male
    iúdicas. 20 100
Non ést flagitium, míhi crede, adulescéntulum
Amáre, neque potáre: non est: néque foris
Effríngere. haec si néque ego neque tu fécimus,
Non síit egestas fácere nos. tu núnc tibi
Id laúdi ducis, quód tum fecisti ínopia? 25 105
Iniúrium est: nam si ésset unde id fíeret,
Facerémus. et tu illúm tuom, si essés homo,
Sinerés nunc facere, dúm per aetatém licet,
Potiús quam, ubi te expectátum eiecissét foras,
Aliéniore aetáte post facerét tamen. 30 110
DE. *(stamping with rage.)* Pro Iúppiter! tu homo ádigis mē
    ad insániam.
Non ést flagitium fácere haec adulescéntulum? MI. *(stop-
    ping his ears.)* Ah!
Auscúlta, ne me obtúndas de hac re saépius.
Tuom fílium dedísti adoptandúm mihi:
Is méus est factus: síquid peccat, Démea, 35 115
Mihi péccat: ego illi máxumam partém fero.
Obsónat, potat, ólet unguenta: dé meo;
Amăt: dábitur a me argéntum, dŭm erit cómmodum.
Vbi nón erit, fortásse excludetúr foras.
Forís effregit; réstituentur: díscidit 40 120
Vestém; resarciétur: et—dis grátia—
Est únde haec fiant, ét adhuc non molésta sunt.

Postrémo aut desine aút cedŏ quemvis árbitrum:
Te plúra in hac re péccare ostendam. **DE.** (*with a groan.*)
  Heí mihi!
Pater ésse disce ab íllis, qui veré sciunt.   45 125
MI. Natúra tu illi páter es, consiliís ego.
DE. (*with a sneer.*) Tun cónsulis quicquam? **MI.** (*impatiently.*) Áh! si pergis, ábiero. (*turning to go away.*)
DE. (*in a tone of remonstrance.*) Sicíne agis? **MI.** An ego tótiens de eadem re aúdiam?
DE. (*petulantly.*) Curae ést mihi. **MI.** Et mihi cúrae est. verum, Démea,
Curémus aequam utérque partem: tu álterum,   50 130
Ego item álterum. nam cúrare ambos própemodum
Repóscere illum est quém dedisti. **DE.** Ah! Mício!
MI. Mihi síc videtur. **DE.** Quíd ístic? (*working himself into a rage.*) si tibi ístúc placet,
Profúndat, perdat, péreat, nil ad me áttinet.
Iam sí verbum unum pósthac— **MI.** (*laying his hand on Demea's shoulder.*) Rursum, Démea,   55 135
Iráscere? **DE.** An non crédis? repeto quém dedi?
(*in an injured tone.*) Aegre ést: alienus nón sum: si obsto
(*Micio makes a deprecating gesture.*)—hem, désino.
(*doggedly.*) Vnúm vis curem, cúro. et est dis grátia,
Quom ita út volo est; isté tuos ipse séntiet
Postérius: nolo in íllum gravius dícere. (*turns on his heel and goes off towards the forum.*)   60 140
MI. Nec níl neque omnia haéc sunt quae dicít: tamen
Non níl molesta haec súnt mihi: sed osténdere
Me aegré pati illi nólui: nam ita ést homo:
Quom pláco, advorsor sédulo et detérreo;
Tamĕn víx humane pátitur: verum si aúgeam   65 145

Aut étiam adiutor sim éius iracúndiae,
Insániam profécto cum illo. etsi Aéschinus
Nonnúllam in hac re nóbis facit iniúriam.
Is núper dixit vélle uxorem dúcere. 151
Sperábam iam defervisse adulescéntiam:
Gaudébam. ecce autem de íntegro: nisi quídquid est
Volŏ scíre atque hominem cónvenire, si ápŭd forum est.
(*exit towards the Forum.*)

ACTVS II.

SC. 1.

SANNIO. AESCHINVS. (PARMENO. PSALTRIA.)

(*Enter Aeschinus, leading the music-girl, attended by his slave Parmeno, and followed by the slave-dealer Sannio, who is in a great state of excitement.*)

SA. (*shouting, with violent gesticulations.*) Óbsecro, populáres,
  ferte mísero atque innocénti auxilium: 155
Súbvenite inopi. **AE.** (*to the music-girl, who, frightened by
  Sannio, makes a hurried movement forward.*) Ótiose;
  (*placing the girl near the door of Micio's house.*)
  núnciam ilico híc consiste.
Quíd respectas? nīl pericli est: númquam, dum ego adero,
  híc te tanget.
SA. (*in a determined tone.*) Égo ístam invitis ómnibus.
AE. (*to the music-girl, composedly.*) Quamquám est scelestus,
  nón committet hódie umquam iterum ut vápulet. 5
SA. (*blustering.*) Aéschine, aūdi! né te ignarum fuísse
  dicas meórum morum, 160

Cómmercor—AE. (*drily*.) Scio. SA. át ita, ut usquam
    fuit fide quisquam óptuma.
Tú quod te postérius purges, hánc iniuriám mihi nolle
Fáctam esse, (*snapping his fingers*.) huius non fáciam. (*in a
    threatening tone*.) crede hoc, égo meum ius pérse-
    quar:
Néque tu verbis sólves umquam, quód mihi re male fé-
    ceris.   10
(*sarcastically*.) Nóvi ego vostra haec 'nóllem factum: iús
    iurandum dábitur, te esse   165
Indígnum iniuria hác,' indignis quom égomet sim acceptús
    modis.
AE. (*to Parmeno*.) Ábi prae strenue ác foris aperi. SA.
    (*endeavouring to obstruct Parmeno*.) Céterum hoc
    nihili facis.
AE. (*to the music-girl*.) Í intro nunciam. SA. (*placing
    himself between the music-girl and the door*.) Át
    enim non sinam. AE. Áccede illuc, Pármeno:
    (*Parmeno moves near Sannio*.)
Nímium istoc abisti: (*placing Parmeno quite close to Sannio*.)
    hic propter húnc adsiste: em! síc volo.   15
Cave núnciam oculos á meis oculis quóquam demoveás
    tuos,   170
Ne móra sit, si innuerím, quin pugnus cóntinuo in mala
    haéreat.
SA. Istúc volo ergo ipsum éxperiri. (*the music-girl at a
    sign from Aeschinus advances towards the door*.)
    AE. (*to Parmeno*.) Hem! sérva: (*to Sannio, who
    seizes hold of the music-girl*.) omitte múlierem.
    (*Aeschinus nods to Parmeno, who gives Sannio a
    hearty cuff on the head*.)
SA. (*putting his hands to his head*.) O fácinus indignúm!

AE. Geminabit nísi caves. (*Parmeno strikes Sannio again.*) **SA.** (*starting back.*) Hei miseró mihi!

AE. (*to Parmeno.*) Non ínnueram: verum ín ístam partem pótius peccató tamen. 20

(*to the music-girl, who goes into the house accompanied by Parmeno.*) I núnciam. **SA.** (*indignantly.*) Quid hóc rei est? regnumne, Aéschine, hic tu póssides? 175

AE. (*drily.*) Si póssiderem, ornátus esses éx tuis virtútibus.

SA. Quid tíbi rei mecum est? **AE.** Níl. **SA.** Quid? nostin quí sim? **AE.** Non desídero.

SA. Tetigín tui quicquam? **AE.** Si áttigisses, férres infortúnium.

SA. (*in a blustering tone.*) Qui tíbi magis licét meam habere, pró qua ego argentúm dedi? 25

Respónde. **AE.** (*quietly.*) Ante aedis nón fecisse erít mélius hic convícium: 180

Nam sí molestus pérgis esse, iam íntro abripiere, átque ibi Vsque ád necem operiére loris. **SA.** (*boiling with indignation.*) Lóris liber! **AE.** Síc erit.

SA. (*crying aloud.*) O hóminem inpurum! hicíne libertatem áiunt esse aequam ómnibus?

AE. (*contemptuously.*) Si sátis iam debacchátus es, scelus, aúdi si vis núnciam. 30

SA. Egŏn débacchatus sum aútem an tu in me? **AE.** Mítte ista atque ad rém redi. 185

SA. Quam rém? quo redeam? **AE.** Iámne me vis dícere id quod ăd te áttinet?

SA. Cupio; aéqui modo aliquíd: tibi enim a me núlla orta est iniúria.

AE. (*sarcastically.*) Nam hercle étiam hoc restat. **SA.** Ílluc quaeso rédĭ, quo coepisti, Aéschine. 190

AE. Minís vigintí tu íllam emisti—quaé res tibi vortát
   male !—   35
Argénti tantum dábitur. SA. Quid? si ego tíbi íllam nolo
   véndere,
Cogés me? AE. Minume. SA. Námque id metui. AE.
   Néque vendundam cénseo,
Quae líbera est: nam ego líberali illam ádsero causá manu.
(*slowly and emphatically*.) Nunc víde utrum vis : argéntum
   accipere an caúsam meditarí tuam.   195
Delíbera hoc, dum egó redeo, scelus. (*exit into Micio's
   house.*) SA. (*wildly*.) Pró supreme Iúppiter !   40
Mínume miror qui ínsanire occípiunt ex iniúria.
Dómŏ me eripuit, vérberavit : me ínvito abduxít meam :
Hómini misero plús quingentos cólaphos infregít mihi.
Ób malefacta haec tántidem emptam póstulat sibi trádier. 200
(*ironically*.) Vérum enim quando béne promeruit, fíat :
   suom ius póstulat.   45
Áge iam cupio, módo si argentum réddat. sed ego hoc -
   háriolor :
Vbi me dixeró dare tanti, téstis faciet ílico,
Véndidisse mé, de argento sómnium : 'mox : crás redi.'
Íd quoque possum férre, modo si réddat, quamquam
   iniúrium est.   205
Vérum cogito íd quod res est : quándo eum quaestum
   incéperis,   50
Áccipiunda et mússitanda iniúria adulescéntium est.
Séd nemo dabít : frustra egomet mécum has rationés puto.

SC. 2.

SYRVS. SANNIO.

(*The door of Micio's house opens. Syrus appears, who speaks to Aeschinus within. Sannio draws somewhat back.*)

SY. (*confidently.*) Tace, égomet conveniam ípsum : cupide
   accípiat faxo atque étiam
,Bene dícat secum esse áctum. (*turns from the door and
   addresses Sannio.*) quid ístuc, Sánnio, est quod
   te aúdio   210
Nescío quid concertásse cŭm ero ? SA. (*in a whining tone.*)
   Númquam vidi iníquius
Certátionem cómparatam, quam haéc hodie inter nós
   fuit :
Ego vápulando, ĭlle vérberando, usque ámbo defessí
   sumus.   5
SY. Tua cúlpa. SA. Quid facerem ? SY. Ádulescenti
   mórem gestum opórtuit.
SA. Qui pótui melius, quí hodie usque os praébui ? SY.
   (*confidentially.*) Age, scis quíd loquar ?   215
Pecúniam in locó neglegere máxumum interdúm est lucrum :
   hui !
Metuísti, si nunc dé tuo iure cóncessisses paúlulum,
Aduléscenti esses mórigeratus, hóminum homō stultís-
   sume,   10
Ne nón tibi istuc faéneraret ? SA. (*doggedly.*) Égo spem
   pretio nón emo.
SY. Numquám rem facies : ábi, inescare néscis homines,
   Sánnio.   220
SA. (*ironically.*) Credo ístuc melius ésse : verum ego
   númquam adeo astutús fui,

Quin quídquid possem mállem auferre pótius in prae-
  séntia.
SY. Age, nóvi tuom animúm: quasi iam usquam tíbi
  sint vigintí minae, 15
Dum huic (*pointing to the house where Aeschinus lives.*)
  óbsequare. praéterea autem te áiunt proficiscí
  Cyprum—SA. (*aside, anxiously.*) Hem!
SY. coemísse hinc quae illuc véheres multa, návem con-
  ductam: hóc scio, 225
Animús tibi pendet. úbi illinc, spero, rédieris tamen, hóc
  ages.
SA. (*vehemently.*) Nusquám pedem. (*aside.*) perii hércle!
  hac illi spe hóc inceperúnt. SY. (*aside, rubbing
  his hands with glee.*) Timet:
Iniéci scrupulum hómini. SA. (*aside.*) O scelera! illúd
  vide, 20
Vt in ípso articulo oppréssit! emptae múlieres
Complúres et item hinc ália quae portó Cyprum. 230
Nisi eo ád mercatum vénio, damnum máxumum est.
Nunc si hóc omitto ac tŭm agam ubi illinc rédiero,
Nil ést; refrixerít res: 'nunc demúm venis? 25
Quor pássu's? ubi eras?' út sit satius pérdere
Quam aut núnc manere tám diu aut tum pérsequi. 235
SY. (*ironically.*) Iamne énumerasti id quód ăd te redi-
  turúm putes?
SA. (*indignantly.*) Hocíne illo dignum est? hócine incipere
  Aéschinum?
Per ŏppréssionem ut hánc mi eripere póstulet? 30
SY. (*aside.*) Labáscit. (*aloud.*) unum hoc hábeo: vidĕ si
  sătĭs placet:
Potiús quam venias ín periclum, Sánnio, 240
Servésne an perdas tótum, dividuóm face.

Minás decem conrádet alicunde. SA. (*wildly*.) Heí mihi!
Etiám de sorte núnc venio in dubiúm miser? 35
Pudét nil? omnis déntis labefecít mihi:
Praetérea colaphis túber est totúm caput: 245
Etiam ínsuper defrúdat? nusquam abeo. SY. (*carelessly*.)
    Vt lubet: (*turning to go away.*)
Numquíd vis quin abeam? SA. (*detaining Syrus*.) Immo
    hercle hoc quaesó, Syre,
Vt ut haéc sunt acta, pótius quam litís sequar, 40
Meum míhi reddatur, sáltem quanti empta ést. (*slipping
    some money into the ready hand of Syrus.*) Syre,
Scio té non usum antehác amicitiá mea: 250
Memorém me dices ésse et gratum. SY. Sédulo
Faciám.—(*breaking off abruptly as he sees Ctesipho.*) sed
    Ctesiphónem video: laétus est
De vírgine. SA. (*anxiously*.) Quid quod te óro? SY.
    Paulispér mane. (*Syrus draws back Sannio to the
    back of the stage.*) 45

SC. 3.

CTESIPHO. SYRUS. (SANNIO.)

(*Ctesipho enters, enraptured at the news of his brother's
    exploit, not seeing Syrus or Sannio.*)

CT. (*joyfully*.) Abs quívis homine, quom ést, opus, bene-
    fícium accipere gaúdeas:
Verum énĭmvero id demúm iuvat, si quem aéquom est
    facere is béne facit. 255
(*with deep emotion.*) O fráter frater, quíd ego nunc te
    laúdem? satís certó scio,

c

Numquam íta magnifice quícquam dicam, id vírtus quin
    superét tua.
Itaque únam hanc rem me habére praeter álios prae-
    cipuam árbitror,   5
Fratrem hómini nemini ésse primarum ártium magís
    príncipem.
SY. (*advancing.*) O Ctésipho! CT. O Syre! Aéschinus
    ubi est? SY. (*pointing to the house.*) Éllum, te
    expectát domi. CT. Hem!   260
SY. Quid ĕst? CT. (*with enthusiasm.*) Quíd sit? illius
    ópera, Syre, nunc vívo: festivóm caput!
Quin ómnia sibi póst putavit ésse prae meo cómmodo,
Maledícta, famam, méum amorem et peccátum in sese
    tránstulit: 10
Nil pótĕst supra. (*a knocking is heard within the door
of Micio's house. Ctesipho, in alarm lest it should
be Demea, turns to hurry away, but is detained by
Syrus, who sees that it is Aeschinus.*) quidnám
    forĭs crepuit? SY. Mánĕ, mane: ipse exít foras.

SC. 4.

AESCHINVS. SANNIO. CTESIPHO. SYRVS.

    (*Aeschinus comes out of Micio's house.*)
AE. Vbi ĕst ílle sacrilegús? SA. (*starting forward.*) Me
    quaerit. núm quidnam effert? (*looking to see if
    Aeschinus is bringing out the money.*) óccidi! 265
Nil vídeo. AE. (*seeing Ctesipho.*) Ehem, opportúne! te
    ipsum quaéro: quid fit, Ctésipho?
In túto est omnis rés: omitte véro tristitiém tuam.

CT. Ego íllam hércle vero omítto, qui quidĕm te hábeam fratrem: (*clasping the hand of Aeschinus.*) O mi Aéschine!
O mí germane! Ah! véreor coram in ós te laudare ámplius,
Ne id ádsentandi mágĭs quam quo habeam grátum facere exístumes. 270
AE. Age inépte, quasi nunc nón norimus nós inter nos, Ctésipho!
Hoc míhi dolet, nos paéne sero scísse et paene in eúm locum
Redísse, ut si omnes cúperent nil tibi póssent auxiliárier.
CT. Pudébat. **AE.** Ah, stultítia est istaec, nón pudor! tam ob párvolam
Rem paéne e patria! túrpe dictu. deós quaeso ut ĭstaec próhibeant. 275
CT. (*in a penitent tone.*) Peccávi. **AE.** (*the brothers embrace; then Aeschinus turns to Syrus.*) Quid aït tándem nobis Sánnio? **SY.** Iam mítis est.
AE. Ego ád forum ibo, ut húnc absolvam: tu íntro ad illam, Ctésipho! (*Aeschinus turns to go to the Forum, Ctesipho into Micio's house.*)
SA. (*apart.*) Syre, ínsta! **SY.** (*aloud to Aeschinus, who is just leaving the stage.*) Eamus: námque hic properat ín Cyprum. **SA.** (*in a determined tone, showing the tip of his finger.*) Ne tám quidem!
Quamvís etiam maneo ótiosus hic. **SY.** Reddetur: né time.
SA. At ut ómne reddat. **SY.** Ómne reddet: tácĕ modŏ ac sequere hác. **SA.** Sequor. (*as Sannio is going off after Aeschinus, Ctesipho re-appears at the door of Micio's house, and calls excitedly to Syrus.*) 280

CT. Heus, heús, Syre! SY. Quid est? CT. Óbsecro
  hercle te, hóminem istum impuríssumum
Quam prímum absolvitóte, ne, si mágis inritatús siet,
Aliqua ád patrem hoc permánet atque ego túm perpetuo
  périerim.
SY. Non fíet, bono animo és: tu cum illa te íntus
  oblecta ínterim,   20
Et léctulos iubē stérni nobis ét parari cétera.   285
Ego iám transacta ré convortam mé domum cum obsónio.
CT. Ita, quaéso: quando hoc béne successit, hílarem hunc
  sumamús diem. (*Ctesipho goes back into Micio's
  house; Syrus hurries off after Aeschinus and
  Sannio.*)

ACTVS III.

SC. 1.

SOSTRATA. CANTHARA.

(*Sostrata comes out of her house, followed by the old nurse
  Canthara.*)

SO. (*anxiously.*) Óbsecro, mea nútrix, quid nunc fíet?
  CA. (*cheerfully.*) Quid fiát rogas?
Recte édepol spero. SO. Módo dolores, méa tu, oc-
  cipiunt prímulum.
CA. Iam núnc times, quasi númquam adfueris, númquam
  tute pépereris?   290

SO. (*wringing her hands.*) Miserám me! neminem hábeo,
   solae súmŭs: Geta autem hic nón adest,
Néc quem ad obstetrícem mittam, néc qui arcessat
   Aéschinum.   5
CA. Pól ĭs quidem iam hic áderit: nam numquam únum
   intermittít diem,
Quin sémper veniat. **SO.** Sólus mearum míseriarum est
   rémedium.
CA. É re nata mélius fieri haud pótuit quam factúm est,
   era,   295
Quándo sic clam núpta est, quod ad illum áttinet potís-
   sumum,
Tálem, tali génere atque animo, nátum ex tanta fámilia. 10
SO. Íta pol est ut dícis: (*raising her clasped hands*) salvos
   nóbis deos quaeso út siet.

SC. 2.

GETA. SOSTRATA. CANTHARA.

(*Geta rushes on, in a state of great excitement, not seeing
Sostrata and Canthara, who withdraw in alarm to the
back of the stage.*)

GE. Nunc íllud est, quod, si ómnes omnia súa consilia
   cónferant,
Atque huíc malo salútem quaerant, aúxili nil ádferant, 300
Quod míhique eraeque fíliaeque eríli est. vae miseró
   mihi!
Tot rés repente círcumvallant, únde. emergi nón·potest,

Vís, egestas, íniustitia, sólitudo, infámia. 5
Hócine saeclum! O scélera! O genera sácrilega! O
 hominem ínpium! (*paces wildly up and down,
 with violent gestures and disordered gait.*)
SO. (*apart.*) Me míseram! quidnam est quód sic video
 tímidum et properantém Getam? 305
GE. (*indignantly.*) quem néque fides, neque iús iurandum,
 néque illum misericórdia
Représsit, neque refléxit, neque quod pártus instabát prope,
Quoi míserae indigne fálsum amorem obtúlerat. SO.
 (*apart.*) Non intéllego 10
Satís quaé loquatur. CA. (*apart.*) Própius, obsecro, ác-
 cedamus, Sóstrata. GE. Ah,
Me míserum! vix sum cómpos animi, ita árdeo ira-
 cúndia. 310
Nil ést quod malim quam illam totam fámiliam darí mi
 óbviam,
Vt ego íram hanc in eos évomam omnem, dum aégritudo
 haec ést recens.
Satís mihi id habeam súpplici, dum illós ulciscar *meó
 modo.* 15
Seni ánimam primum extínguerem ipsi, qui illud pro-
 duxít scelus:
Tum autém Syrum inpulsórem, vah! quibus illum lacer-
 arém modis! 315
Sublímem medium prímum arríperem et cápite in terram
 státuerem,
Vt cérebro dispergát viam.
Ádulescenti ipsi ériperem oculos, póst haec praecipitém
 darem: 20
(*with violent gestures.*) Céteros ruerem, ágerem, raperem,
 túnderem et prostérnerem.

(*exhausted and gasping from the vehemence of his passion.*)
Sed césso eram hoc malo ínpertiri própere?
(*hurries towards Sostrata's house*). SO. Revo-
cemús.—Geta! .GE. (*impatiently, without look-
ing round.*) Hem! 320
Quísquis es, sine me. SO. Égo sum Sostrata. GE.
(*turning hastily.*) Úbi ea est? te ipsam quaérito,
Te éxpecto: oppido ópportune te óbtulisti mi óbviam.
(*Geta's agitation becomes so great that he can scarcely
speak.*) Éra!—SO. Quid est? quid trépidas? GE.
Hei mihi! (*walking wildly up and down*). SO.
Quíd festinas, mí Geta? 25
Ánimam recipe. GE. Prórsus—SO. Quíd ístuc 'prórsus'
ergo est? GE. périimus:
Áctum est. SO. Eloquere, óbsecro te, quíd sit. GE.
Iam—SO. Quid 'iám,' Geta? 325
GE. Aéschinus—SO. Quid is érgo? GE. alienus ést ab
nostra fámilia. SO. (*with a bitter cry.*) Hem!
Périi! (*she buries her face in her hands, unable to speak for
some moments; then asks in a broken voice*) qua
re? GE. Amáre occepit áliam. SO. Vae mise-
raé mihi!
GE. Néque id occulte fért, ab domino eam ípsus eripuít
palam. 30
SO. Sátine hoc certum est? GE. Cértum: hisce oculis
égomet vidi, Sóstrata, SO. (*with a cry of despair.*) Ah,
Me míseram! quid iam crédas? aut quoi crédas? nostrumne Aéschinum? 330
Nostrám vitam omnium, ín quo nostrae spés opesque
omnés sitae
Eránt! quí sine hac iurábat se unum númquam victurúm diem?

Qui se ín sui gremió positurum púerum dicebát patris? 35
Ita óbsecraturum, út liceret hánc sibi ŭxorem agnóscere?
(*bursts into tears.*)
GE. Era, lácrumas mitte ac pótius quod ad hanc rem
óp us est porro próspice :   335
Patiámurne an narrémus quoipiam? CA. (*in a tone of indignant expostulation.*) Aú, au, mí homo, sánun es?
An hŏc próferendum tíbi videtur úsquam? GE. Mihi
quidĕm nón placet.
Iam prímum illum alieno ánimo a nobis ésse res ipsa índicat.   40
Nunc si hóc palam proférimus, ille infítias ibit, sát scio :
Tua fáma et gnatae víta in dubium véniet. tum si
máxume   340
Fateátur, quŏm amet áliam, non est útile hanc illí dari.
Quaprópter quoquo pácto tacito est ópus. SO. Ah, minume géntium!
Non fáciam. GE. Quid ages? SO. (*with determination.*)
Próferam. CA. (*alarmed.*) Hem! mea Sóstrata,
vidĕ quám rem agis.   45
SO. Peióre res locó non potis est ésse quam in quo núnc
sita est.   344
Si infítias ibit, téstis mecum est ánulus quem amíserat.
Postrémo quando ego cónscia mihi sum, á me culpam
esse hánc procul,   50
Neque prétium neque rem ullam íntercessisse ílla aut me
indignám, Geta,
Expériar. GE. Quid ístic? cédo ut melius dícas. SO.
Tu, quantúm potes*t*,   350
Abi ătque Hégioni, cógnato eius, rem énarrato omnem
órdine :

Nam is nóstro Simuló fuit summus ét nos coluit máxume.
GE. Nam hercle álius nemo réspicit nos. (*exit Geta.*) SO.
       Própera tu, mea Cánthara, 55
Curre, óbstetricem arcésse, ut, quom opŭs sit, ne ín mora
       nobís siet. (*Canthara hurries off, and Sostrata
       returns to her house.*)

SC. 3.

DEMEA. SYRVS.

(*Demea enters from the Forum, in great agitation.*)
DE. Dispérii! Ctesiphónem audivi fílium   355
Vná fuisse in ráptione cum Aéschino.
Id mísero restat míhi mali, si illúm potest,
Qui aliquoí rei est, etiam eum ád nequitiem addúcere.
Vbi ego íllum quaeram? crédo, abduxit Aéschinus   5
Aliquó: persuasit ílle inpurus, sát scio. (*he looks round.*)
Sed eccúm Syrum ire vídeo: iam hinc scibo úbi siet. 361
Atque hércle hic de grege íllo est: si me sénserit
Eum quaéritare, númquam dicet cárnufex.
Non óstendam id me vélle. (*Syrus enters talking aloud, but
       pretending not to see Demea.*) SY. Omnem rem
       módo seni   10
Quo pácto haberet énarramus órdine.   365
Nil quícquam vidi laétius. DE. (*aside.*) Pro Iúppiter!
Hominís stultitiam! SY. Cónlaudavit fílium:
Mihi, qui íd dedissem cónsilium, egit grátias.
DE. Disrúmpor. (*aside.*) SY. Argentum ádnumeravit ílico:
Dedít praeterea in šúmptum dimidiúm minae: 370
Id dístributum sáne est ex senténtia. DE. (*aside, ironi-
       cally.*) Hem!

Huic mándes, siquid récte curatúm velis. (*advances towards Syrus.*)

SY. (*with affected surprise.*) Ehĕm Démea! haud aspéxeram te: quíd agitur?

DE. Quid agátur? (*ironically.*) vostram néqueo mirarí satis Rationem. **SY.** (*apologetically.*) Est hercle inépta,—ne dicám dolo, 375

Absúrda. (*calling into the house.*) piscis céteros purgá, Dromo:

Congrum ístum maxumum ín aqua sinito lúdere

Tantísper: ubi ego rédiero, exossábitur:

Priŭs nólo. **DE.** Haecine flagítia!—(*interrupting.*) **SY.** Mihi quidĕm nón placent, 25

Et clámo saepe. (*calling into the house.*) sálsamenta haec, Stéphanio, 380

Fac mácerentur púlchre. **DE.** Di vostrám fidem!

Vtrúm studione id síbi habet, an laudí putat

Fore, sí perdiderit gnátum? vae miseró mihi!

Vidére videor iám diem illum, quom hínc egens 30

Profúgiet aliquo mílitatum. **SY.** (*with mock solemnity.*) O Démea! 385

Istúc est sapere, nón quod ante pedés modo est

Vidére, sed etiam ílla quae futúra sunt

Prospícere. **DE.** Quid? Ístaec iám penes vos psáltria est?

SY. (*with affected shame.*) Ellam íntus. **DE.** (*indignantly.*) Eho! ăn domí est habiturus? **SY.** Crédo, ut est 35

Deméntia. **DE.** Haecine fíeri! **SY.** Inepta lénitas 390

Patris ét facilitas práva. **DE.** Fratris mé quidem

Pudét pigetque. **SY.** Nímium inter vos, Démea—

Non, quía ades praesens, díco hoc—pernimium ínterest.

Tu, quántus quantu's, (*bowing low*) níl nisi sapiéntia es, 40

Ílle sómnium. sinerés vero illum tú tuom   395
Facere haéc? **DE.** Sinerem illum? aut nón sex totis
    ménsibus
Prius ólfecissem, quam ílle quicquam coéperet?
SY. Vigilántiam tuam tú mihi narras? **DE.** Síc siet
Modo ŭt núnc est, quaeso. **SY.** Vt quísque suom volt
    ésse, ita est.   45
DE. Quid eúm? vidistin hódie? **SY.** Tuomne fílium? 400
(*aside.*) Abigam húnc rus. (*aloud.*) iam dudum áliquid
    ruri agere árbitror.
DE. Satĭn scís ibi esse? **SY.** Oh! qui égomet produxi.
    DE. Óptume est;
Metuí ne haereret híc. **SY.** Atque iratum ádmodum.
DE. Quid aútem? **SY.** Adortus iúrgio est fratrem ápŭd
    forum   50
De psáltria istac. **DE.** Aín vero? **SY.** Ah, nil réti-
    cuit.   405
Nam ut númerabatur fórte argentum, intérvenit
Homo de ínproviso; coépit clamare 'o Aéschine,
Haecíne flagitia fácere te! haec te admíttere
Indígna genere nóstro!' **DE.** Oh! lacrumo gaúdio.   56
SY. 'Non tu hóc argentum pérdis, sed vitám tuam.' 410
DE. Salvós sit, spero: est símilis maiorúm suom. **SY.**
    (*with ironical admiration.*) Hui!
DE. Syre, praéceptorum plénust istorum ílle. **SY.** Phy!
(*bowing to Demea.*) Domi hábuit unde dísceret. **DE.** Fit
    sédulo:
Nil praétermitto: cónsuefacio: dénique   60
Inspícere tamquam in spéculum in vitas ómnium   415
Iubeo, átque ex aliis súmere exemplúm sibi.
'Hoc fácito.' **SY.** Recte sáne. **DE.** 'Hoc fugito.' **SY.**
    Cállide.

DE. 'Hoc laúdi est.' **SY.** Istaec rés est. **DE.** 'Hoc vitió datur.'
SY. Probíssume. **DE.** Porro aútem—**SY.** (*interrupting.*)
    Non hercle ótium est   65
Nunc mi aúscultandi. píscis ex senténtia   420
Nactús sum: hi mihi ne córrumpantur caútio est:
Nam id nóbis tam flagítium est quam illa, Démea,
Non fácere vobis, quaé modo dixti: et, quód queo,
Consérvis ad eundem ístunc praecipió modum: 70   424
(*with à parody of Demea's tones and gestures.*) 'Hoc sálsum
    est, hoc adústum est, hoc lautúm est parum:
Illúd recte: iterum síc memento:' sédulo
Moneó, quae possum pró mea sapiéntia:
Postrémo támquam in spéculum in patinas, Démea,
Inspícere iubeo et móneo quid facto úsŭs sit.   75
Inépta haec esse, nós quae facimus, séntio: 430
Verúm quid facias? út homo est, ita morém geras.
(*turning to go.*) Numquíd vis? **DE.** (*surlily.*) Mentem
    vóbis meliorém dari.
SY. Tu rús hinc ibis? **DE.** Récta. **SY.** Nam quid tu
    híc agas,
Vbi síquid bene praecípias, nemo obtémperet? (*exit Syrus
    into Micio's house.*)   80
DE. Ego véro hinc abeo, quándo is, quam ob rem huc
    véneram,   435
Rus ábiit: illum cúro unum, ille ad me áttinet:
Quando íta volt frater, de ístoc ipse víderit. (*turning to go.*)
Sed quís íllic est, quem vídeo procul? estne Hégio
Tribúlis noster? sí satís cerno, is ĕst hércle: vah!   85
Homo amícus nobis iam índe a puero: dí boni,   440
Ne ílliús modi iam mágna nobis cívium
Penúria est antíqua virtute ác fide.

Haud cíto mali quid órtum ex hoc sit públice.
Quam gaúdeo! ubi etiam húius generis réliquias 90
Restáre video, vívere etiam núnc lubet. 445
Oppériar hominem hic, út salutem et cónloquar.

SC. 4.

HEGIO. GETA. DEMEA.

(*Hegio enters from the Forum, in conversation with Geta, not seeing Demea, who retires to the back of the stage.*)

HE. (*indignantly.*) Pro di ínmortales, fácinus indignúm,
  Geta!
Quid nárras? GE. Sic est fáctum. HE. Ex illan fámilia
Tam inlíberale fácinus esse ortum! O Aéschine,
Pol haúd paternum istúc dedisti. DE. (*aside.*) Vídĕlicet 450
De psáltria hac audívit: id illi núnc dolet 5
Aliéno, pater eius níhili pendit: heí mihi,
Vtinam híc prope adesset álicubi atque audíret haec.
HE. Nisi fácient quae illos aéquom est, haud sic aúferent.
GE. In té spes omnis, Hégio, nobís sita est: 455
Te sólum habemus, tu és patronus, tú pater: 10
Illé tibi moriens nós commendavít senex:
Si déseris tu, périimus. HE. Cavĕ díxeris:
Neque fáciam neque me sátis pie̱ posse árbitror.
DE. (*aside.*) Adíbo. salvere Hégionem plúrimum 460
Iubeo. HE. (*stiffly.*) Óh! te quaerebam ípsum: salve,
  Démea. 15
DE. Quid aútem? HE. Maior fílius tuos Aéschinus,
Quem frátri adoptandúm dedisti, néque boni

Neque líberalis fúnctus officium ést viri.
DE. Quid ístúc est? **HE.** Nostrum amícum noras Símu-
    lum   465
Aequálem? **DE.** Quid ni? **HE.** Fíliam eius vírginem   20
Clam dúxit. **DE.** Hem! **HE.** Manĕ: nóndum audisti,
    Démea,
Quod ést gravissumum. **DE.** Án quicquam est etiam ám-
    plius?
HE. Vero ámplius: nam hoc quídĕm ferundum aliquó
    modo est: 469
Humánum est. post id fáctum, ad matrem vírginis   25
Venit ípsus ultro, lácrumans, orans, óbsecrans,
Fidém dans, iurans sé illam ducturúm domum.
Ignótum est, tacitum est, créditum est. at vírgini
Dum pártus instat, (átque hic mensis décimus est),   475
Ílle bónŭs vir nobis psáltriam, si dís placet,   30
Parávit, quicum vívat: illam déserit.
DE. Pro cérto tu istaec dícis? **HE.** Mater vírginis
In médio est, ipsa vírgo, res ipsa, híc Geta
Praetérea, ut captus ést servorum, nón malus   480
Neque inérs: alit illas, sólus omnem fámiliam   35
Susténtat: hunc abdúce, vinci, quaére rem.
GE. Immo hércle extorque, nísi ita factum est, Démea;
Postrémo non negábit: coram ipsúm cedo.
DE. Pudét: nec quid agam, néc quid huic dicám, scio. 485
HE. Illaéc fidem nunc vóstram inplorat, Démea,
Quod vós vis cogit, íd voluntate ínpetret.   490
Haec prímum ut fiant deós quaeso ut vobís decet.   ·45
Sin áliter animus vóster est, ego, Démea,
Summá vi defendam hánc atque illum mórtuom.
(*with deep feeling.*) Cognátus mihi erat: úna a pueris pár-
    volis

Sumus éducti : una sémper militiae ét domi   495
Fuimús : paupertatem úna pertulimús gravem.   50
Quaprópter nitar, fáciam, experiar, dénique
Animám relinquam pótius quam illas déseram.
Quid míhi respondes ? DE. Frátrem conveniam, Hégio.
HE. Sed, Démea, hoc tu fácito cum animo cógites,   500
Quam vós facillume ágitis, quam estis máxume   55
Poténtes, dites, fórtunati, nóbiles,
Tam máxume vos aéquo animo aequa nóscere
Opórtet, si vos vóltis perhiberí probos. (*turns to depart.*)
DE. Redíto : fient quaé fieri aequom est ómnia.   505
HE. Decét te facere. Géta, duc me intro ad Sóstratam.
    (*exeunt Hegio and Geta into the house of Sostrata.*)
DE. Non me índicente haec fíunt : utinam hic sít modo
Defúnctum : verum nímia illaec licéntia
Profécto evadet ín aliquod magnúm malum.
Ibo ác requiram frátrem, ut in eum haec évomam. (*exit
    Demea to the Forum.*)   510

SC. 5.

HEGIO.

(*Hegio appears at the door of Sostrata's house, and speaks to
her within.*)
Bono ánimo fac sis, Sóstrata, et istam, quód potes,
Fac cónsolere. ego Mícionem, si ápŭd forum est,
Convéniam, atque, ut res gésta est, narrabo órdine :
Si est, *is* facturus út sit officiúm suom,
Faciát : sin aliter de hác re est eius senténtia,   5   515
Respóndeat mi, ut quíd agam quam primúm sciam. (*exit
    to the Forum.*)

ACTVS IV.

SC. 1.

CTESIPHO. SYRVS.

(*Ctesipho comes out of Micio's house in conversation with Syrus.*)

CT. Aín patrem hinc abísse rus? **SY.** Iam dúdum.
    CT. (*pleadingly.*) Dic, sodés. **SY.** Apŭd villam est:
Núnc quom maxume óperis aliquid fácere credo. **CT.**
    Vtinám quidem!
Quod cúm salute eius fíat, ita se. défetigarít velim,
Vt tríduo hoc perpétuo prorsum e lécto nequeat súr-
    gere.   520
SY. Ita fíat, et istoc síquid potis est réctius. **CT.** Ita:
    nam húnc diem   5
Miseré nimis cupio, ut coépi, perpetuom ín laetitia dégere.
Ét illud rus nulla ália causa tám male odi, nísi quia prope
    est.
Quód si abesset lóngius,
Priús nox oppressísset illic, quam húc revorti pósset ite-
    rum.   525
Núnc ubi me illic nón videbit, iam húc recurret, sát scio: 10
Rogitábit mĕ, ubi fúerim: 'ego hodie tóto non vidí
    die:'
Quid dícam? **SY.** Nilne in ménte est? **CT.** Numquam
    quícquam. **SY.** (*with some contempt.*) Tanto né-
    quior.
Cliéns, amicus, hóspes nemo est vóbis? **CT.** Sunt: quid
    póstea?

SY. Hisce ópera ut data sit. **CT.** (*indignantly.*) Quaé non data sit? nón potest fierí. **SY.** Potest. 530
CT. (*yielding.*) Intérdiu: sed si híc pernocto, caúsae quid dicám, Syre? 15
SY. Vah! quám vellem etiam nóctu amicis óperam mos essét dari.
Quin tu ótiosus és: ego illius sénsum pulchre cálleo.
Quom férvit maxumé, tam placidum quási ovem reddo.
CT. Quó modo?
SY. Laudárier te audít lubenter: fácio te apud illúm deum: 535
Virtútes narro. **CT.** (*with unaffected astonishment.*) Meás?
SY. Tuas: homini flico lacrumaé cadunt 20
Quasi púero gaudio:—(*looking round he sees Demea approaching.*) ém tibi autem! **CT.** Quídnam est? **SY.** Lupus in fábula.
CT. Pater ést? **SY.** *Is* ipse est. **CT.** (*in the greatest alarm.*) Sýre, quid agimus? **SY.** (*impatiently; pushing Ctesipho into the door of Micio's house.*) Fúge modo intro, ego vídero.
CT. Siquíd rogabit, núsquam tu me: audístin? **SY.** Potin ut désinas? (*Ctesipho hides behind the door.*)

SC. 2.

DEMEA. CTESIPHO. SYRVS.

(*Demea enters without seeing Syrus, who keeps close to the door of Micio's house*).

DE. Ne égo homo infelix! prímum fratrem núsquam invenio géntium: 540

Praéterea autem, dum íllum quaero, a vílla mercenárium
Vídi: is filiúm negat esse rúri: nec quid agám scio.
CT. (*putting his head out of the door, and whispering to Syrus.*)
    Sýre! SY. (*apart.*) Quid est? CT. (*apart.*) Men
    quaérit? SY. (*apart.*) Verum. CT. (*apart.*) Périi!
    SY. (*apart.*) Quin tu animó bono es.
DE. Quíd hŏc, malum, infelícitatis? néqueo satĭs decér-
    nere: 5
Nísi me credo huic ésse natum reí, ferundis míseriis. 545
Prímus sentió mala nostra: prímus rescisco ómnia:
Prímus porro obnúntio; aegre sólus, siquid fít, fero.
SY. (*aside.*) Rídeo hunc: primum aít se scire: is sólus
    nescit ómnia.
DE. Núnc redeo: si fórte frater rédierit visó. CT.
    (*whispering as before.*) Syre!   10
Óbsecro, vidĕ ne ílle huc prorsus se ínruat. SY. (*apart.*)
    Etiám taces?   550
Égo cavebo. CT. (*apart.*) Númquam hercle hodie ego
    ístuc committám tibi:
Nám me iam in cellam áliquam cum illa cóncludam: id
    tutíssumum est.
SY. (*apart.*) Áge, tamen ego hunc ámovebo. (*Ctesipho dis-
    appears, and Syrus comes hastily forward, pretend-
    ing not to notice Demea.*) DE. Séd ĕccum scele-
    ratúm Syrum.
SY. (*speaking, so as to be overheard, in a whining tone.*)
    Nón hercle hic quidém durare quísquam, si sic
    fít, potest.   15
Scíre equidem voló, quot mihi sint dómini: quae haec est
    míseria!   555
DE. (*aside.*) Quíd ĭlle gannit? quíd volt? (*aloud.*) quid aĭs,
    bóne vir? est fratér domi?

SY. (*angrily.*) Quíd, malum, 'bone vír' mihi narras? équidem perii. **DE.** Quíd tibi est?

SY. Rógitas? Ctesiphó me pugnis míserum et istam psáltriam
Vsque occidit. **DE.** Hém! quid narras? **SY.** Ém! (*pretending to show the inside of his lip.*) vide ŭt discidít labrum. 20 559

DE. Quam ób rem? **SY.** Me inpulsóre hanc (*pointing to the house*) emptam esse aít. **DE.** (*suspiciously.*) Non tu eum rus hínc modo
Próduxe aibas? **SY.** Fáctum: verum vénit post insániens:
Níl pepercit. nón puduisse vérberare hominém senem! Quem égo modo puerúm tantillum in mánibus gestaví meis.

DE. Laúdo: Ctesiphó, patrissas: ábi, virum te iúdico. 25
SY. Laúdas? ne ille cóntinebit pósthac, si sapiét, manus. 565
DE. Fórtiter! **SY.** (*ironically.*) Perquám, quia miseram múlierem et me sérvolum,
Quí referire nón audebam, vícit: hui, perfórtiter!
DE. Nón potuit meliús. idem quod ego, sénsit te esse huic reí caput.
Séd ěstne frater íntus? **SY.** (*sulkily.*) Non est. **DE.** Vbi íllum inveniam cógito. 30

SY. Scío ubi sit, verum hódie numquam mónstrabo. **DE.** Hem! quid aís? **SY.** Ita. 570
DE. (*shaking his stick at Syrus.*) Díminuetur tíbi quidem iam cérebrum. **SY.** At nomen néscio
Íllius hominis, séd locum novi úbi sit. **DE.** Dic ergó locum.
SY. Nóstin porticum apúd macellum hac deórsum? (*pointing.*) **DE.** Quid ni nóverim?

SY. Praéterito hac récta platea súrsum. ubi eo véneris, 35
Clívos deorsum vórsum est: hac te praécipitato: póstea 575
Ést ad hanc manúm sacellum: ibi ángiportum própter est.
DE. Quódnam? SY. Illi ubi etiám caprificus mágna
  est. DE. Novi. SY. Hac pérgito.
DE. (*after some consideration.*) Íd quidem angipórtum non
  est pérvium. SY. Verum hércle: vah!
Cénsen hominem me éssc? erravi: in pórticum rursúm
  redi: 40
Sáne hac multo própius ibis ét minor est errátio. 580
Scín Cratini huius dítis aedis? DE. Scío. SY. Vbi eas
  praetérieris,
Ád sinistram hac récta platea; ubi ád Dianae véneris,
Íto ad dextram: príús quam ad portam vénias, apud ipsúm
  lacum,
Ést pistrilla et éxadvorsum fábrica: ibi est. DE. (*doubtfully.*)
  Quid íbi facit? 45
SY. Léctulos in sóle ilignis pédibus faciundós dedit. 585
DE. Vbi potetis vós: bene sane. séd cesso ad eum pér-
  gere? (*exit hurriedly.*)
SY. (*laughing.*) Í sane: ego te exércebo hodie, ut dígnus
  es, silicérnium!
(*turning to the audience.*) Aéschinus odióse cessat: prándium
  corrúmpitur:
Ctésipho autem in amóre est totus. égo iam prospiciám
  mihi: 50
Nám iam adibo, atque únumquicquid, quód quidem erit
  bellíssumum, 590
Cárpam, et cyathos sórbillans paulátim hunc producám
  diem. (*exit into Micio's house.*)

SC. 3.

MICIO. HEGIO.

(*Micio and Hegio enter from the Forum in conversation.*)
MI. (*in a deprecating tone.*) Ego in hác re nil repério, quam
    ob rem laúder tantopere, Hégio.
Meum offícium facio: quód peccatum a nóbis ortum est,
    córrigo.
Nisi sí me in illo crédidisti esse hóminum numéro, qui íta
    putant,
Sibi fíeri iniuriam últro, si quam fécere ipsi expóstules,   595
Et últro accusant: íd quia non est á me factum, agís
    grátias?   5
HE. Ah! mínume: numquam te áliter atque es ín animum
    induxí meum.
Sed quaéso ut una mécum ad matrem vírginis eas, Mício,
Atque ístaec eadem quaé mihi dixti túte dicas múlieri,
Suspítionem hanc própter fratrem eius ésse et illam psál-
    triam.   600
MI. Si ita aéquom censes aút si ita opus est fácto, eamus.
    HE. Béne facis: 10
Nam et ílli iam relevábis animum, quaé dolore ac míseria
Tabéscit, et tuo ófficio fueris fúnctus. sed si alitér putas,
Egomét narrabo quaé mihi dixti. **MI.** Ímmo ego ibo.
    HE. Béne facis:
(*with feeling.*) Omnés, quibús res sunt mínús secundae,
    mágis sunt nescio quó modo   605
Suspítiosi: ad cóntumeliam ómnia accipiúnt magis: 15
Proptér suam inpoténtiam se sémper credunt claúdier.
Quaprópter te ipsum púrgare ipsi córam placabílius est.
MI. Et récte et verum dícis. **HE.** Sequere me érgo hac
    intro. **MI.** Máxume. (*exeunt into Sostrata's house.*)

SC. 4.

AESCHINVS.

(Enter Aeschinus from the Forum in a state of deep dejection.)

Discrúcior ánimi!	610 *a*
Hocíne de inprovisó mali	610 *b*

Mi obicí tantum, ut neque quíd me faciam néc quid agam
    certúm siet!

Mémbra metu debília sunt:	612 *a*
Animús timore obstípuit:	612 *b*

Péctore consístere nil cónsilï quit.
Vah! quó modo hac me expédiam turba? tánta nunc
    Suspítio de me íncidit: 615
    Néque ea inmerito: Sóstrata
Crédit mihi me psáltriam hanc emísse: id anus mi indícium
    fecit.
Nám ut hinc forte ea ad óbstetricem erăt míssa, ubi eam
    vidi, ílico   10
Accédo: rogito, Pámphila quid agát, iam partus ádsiet,
Eone óbstetricem arcéssat. illa exclámat 'abi, abi iam,
    Aéschine!   620
Satïs diú dedisti vérba: sat adhuc túa nos frustratá est
    fides.'
"Hem, quíd ístuc, obsecro," ínquam, "est?" 'valeas,
    hábeas illam quaé placet.'
Sensi ílico id illas súspicari: séd me reprehendí tamen, 15
Nequíd de fratre gárrulae illi dícerem ac fierét palam.
Núnc quid faciam? dícam fratris ésse hanc? quod minume
    ést opus   625
Vsquam efferri: ac mítto: fieri pótis est ut nequa éxeat.
Ípsum id metuo ut crédant: tot concúrrunt veri símilia:

Égomet rapui : ipse égomet solvi argéntum : ad me abductá
    est domum.   20
Haéc adeo mea cúlpa fateor fíeri. non me hanc rém patri,
Út ut erat gesta, índicasse! exórassem ut eam dúcerem. (*he
    hides his face in his hands for a few moments, then
    speaks with determination.*)   630
Céssatum usque adhúc est : nunc porro, Aéschine, exper-
    gíscere :
Núnc hoc primum est : ád íllas ibo, ut púrgem me. acce-
    dam ád foris. (*advances towards the door, but stops
    half-way.*)
Périi! horresco sémper, ubi pultáre hasce occipió miser. 25
(*summoning up his courage.*) Heús, heus! Aeschinús ego
    sum. (*goes to the door and knocks loudly.*) aperite
    áliquis actutum óstium. (*the door opens.*)   634
Pródit nescio quís : concedam huc. (*retires.*)

SC. 5.

MICIO. AESCHINVS.

(*Micio comes out of the house, and, unheard by Aeschinus,
speaks through the door to Sostrata within.*)

                    MI. Íta uti dixi, Sóstrata,
Fácite : ego Aeschinúm conveniam, ut quó modo acta haec
    sínt sciat. (*turning towards Aeschinus.*)
Séd quis ostium hóc pultavit ? **AE.** (*aside.*) Páter hercle
    est, perii! **MI.** Aéschine!
AE. (*aside.*) Quid huïc híc negoti est? **MI.** túne has pepu-
    listí foris ? (*pauses for a reply.*)
(*aside.*) Tacĕt. quór non ludo hunc áliquantisper ? mélius
    est,   5

Quandóquidem hoc numquam mi ípse voluit dícere. 640
(*to Aeschinus.*) Nil míhi respondes? **AE.** (*confused.*) Nón
    equidem istas, quód sciam.
MI. Ita: nám mirabar, quíd hïc negoti essét tibi. (*pauses,
    closely watching Aeschinus, who has half turned
    away.*)
(*aside, joyfully.*) Erúbuit: salva rés est. **AE.** (*trying to hide
    his anxiety.*) Dic sodés, pater,
Tibi véro quid ïstic ést rei? **MI.** (*carelessly.*) Nil míhi
    quidem. 10
Amícus quidam me á foro abduxít modo 645
Huc ádvocatum síbi. **AE.** Quid? **MI.** Ego dicám tibi:
Habitánt hic quaedam múlieres paupérculae:
Vt opínor has non nósse te, et certó scio:
Neque ením diu huc migrárunt. **AE.** Quid tum póstea? 15
MI. Virgo ést cum matre. **AE.** Pérge. **MI.** Haec virgo
    orba ést patre: 650
Hic méus amicus ílli genere est próxumus:
Huic léges cogunt núbere hanc. **AE.** (*aside, but overheard
    by Micio.*) Perií! **MI.** Quid est?
AE. (*much agitated.*) Nil: récte: perge. **MI.** Is vénit ut
    secum ávehat:
Nam habitát Mileti. **AE.** (*with horror.*) Hem! vírginem
    ut secum ávehat? 20
MI. Sic ést. **AE.** Miletum usque óbsecro? **MI.** Ita.
    AE. (*aside.*) Animó male est. 655
(*aloud.*) Quid ípsaé? quid aiunt? **MI.** Quíd íllas censes?
    níl enim.
Comménta mater ést, esse ex alió viro
Nesció quo puerum nátum: neque eum nóminat:
Prióreni esse illum, nón oportere huíc dari. 25
AE. Eho! nónne haec iusta tíbi videntur póst ea? 660

MI. Non. **AE.** Óbsecro non? án íllam hinc abducét,
   pater?
MI. Quid íllám ni abducat? **AE.** (*vehemently.*) Fáctum a
   vobis dúriter,
Inmísericorditérque, atque etiam, si ést, pater,
Dicéndum magis apérte, inliberáliter. 30
MI. (*with affected surprise.*) Quam ob rém? **AE.** Rogas
   me? quíd ílli tandem créditis 665
Fore ánimi misero, qui ílla consuevít prior?
Qui infélix haud scio an íllam misere núnc amet,
Quom hanc síbi videbit praésens praesentem éripi,
Abdúci ab oculis? fácinus indignúm pater! 35
MI. Qua rátione istuc? quís despondit? quís dedit? 670
Quoi, quándo nupsit? aúctor his rebús quis est?
Quor dúxit alienam? **AE.** Án sedere opórtuit
Domí vírginem tam grándem, dum cognátus hinc
Illínc veniret éxpectantem? haec, mí pater, 40
Te dícere aequom fúit et id deféndere. 675
MI. Ridículum! advorsumne íllum causam dícerem,
Quoi véneram advocátus? sed quid ísta, Aéschine,
Nostra? aút quid nobis cum íllis? abeamús. (*Aeschinus
   bursts into tears.*) quid est?
Quíd lacrumas? **AE.** (*sobbing.*) Pater, óbsecro, ausculta.
   MI. Aéschine, audivi ómnia 45
Ét scio: nam té amo: quo magís quaé agís curae súnt
   mihi. 680
AE. Íta velim me prómerentem amés, dum vivas, mí pater,
Vt me hoc delictum ádmisisse in me, íd mihi vehementér
   dolet,
Ét me tui pudét. (*he buries his face.*) **MI.** Credo hercle:
   nam íngenium noví tuom
Líberale: séd vereor ne indíligens nimiúm sies. 50

Ín qua civitáte tandem te árbitrare vívere? 685
Vírginem clam dúxisti, quam nón ius fuerat dúcere.
Iam íd peccatum prímum magnum, *mágnum*, at humanúm tamen:
Fécere alii saépe item boni. ăt póstquam id evenít, cedo,
Númquid circumspéxti? aut numquid túte prospextí tibi, 55
Quíd fieret? qua fíeret? si te mi ípsum puduit próloqui, 690
Quá resciscerem? haéc dum dubitas, ménses abierúnt decem.
Pródidisti et te ét íllam miseram et gnátum, quod quidem ín té fuit.
Quíd? credebas dórmienti haec tíbi confecturós deos?
Ét íllam sine tua ópera in cubiculum íri deductúm domum? 60
Nólim ceterárum rerum té socordem eodém modo. (*changing his tone, and laying his hand on Aeschinus' shoulder, who has turned away overcome with shame.*) 695
Bóno animo es, ducés uxorem hanc. **AE.** (*starting.*) Hém! **MI.** Bono, inquam, animo és. **AE.** (*imploringly.*) Pater,
Óbsecro, nunc lúdis tu me? **MI.** Égo te? quam ob rem? **AE.** Néscio:
Quía tam misere hoc ésse cupio vérum, eo vereór magis.
MI. Ábí domum ac deos cómprecare, ut úxorem arcessás: abi. 65
AE. Quíd? iam uxorem? **MI.** Iám. **AE.** Iam? **MI.** Iam quantúm potest. **AE.** (*with deep feeling.*) Di mé, pater, 700
Ómnes oderínt, ni magís te quam óculos nunc ego amó meos.

IV. 5. 68–6. 6.   ADELPHI.   43

MI. Quíd? quam illam?   **AE.** Aeque.   **MI.** Pérbenigne.
   AE. (*with a sudden start.*) Quíd? ïlle ubi est
   Milésius?
MI. Périit, abiit, návem ascendit; séd quor cessas? **AE.**
   Ábï, pater,
Tú potius deos cómprecare: nám tibi eos certó scio,   70
Quó vir melior múlto es quăm ego, obtémperaturós
   magis. (*falls upon Micio's neck.*)   705
MI. Égo eo intro, ut quae opŭs súnt parentur: tú fac ŭt
   dixi, sí sapis. (*exit into his house.*)
AE. Quid hŏc ést negoti? hoc ést patrem esse aut hóc
   est filium ésse?
Si fráter aut sodális esset, quí magís morem géreret?
Hic nón amandus? hícine non gestándus in sinu ést?
   hem!   75 709
Itaque ádeo magnam mi ínicit sua cómmoditate cúram,
Ne fórte inprudens fáciam quod nolít: sciens cavébo.
Sed césso ire intro, né morae meis núptiis egomét siem.
   (*exit into Micio's house.*)

SC. 6.

DEMEA.

(*Demea comes on weary and footsore.*)

DE. Deféssus sum ambulándo: ut, Syre, te cúm tua
Monstrátione mágnus perdat Iúppiter! (*shaking his stick.*)
Perréptavi usque omne óppidum: ad portam, ád lacum, 715
Quo nón? neque ïllic fabrica úlla erat, nec frátrem homo
Vidísse se aibat quísquam. nunc veró domi   5
Certum óbsidere est úsque, donec rédierit. (*goes towards
   the house.*)

SC. 7.

DEMEA. MICIO.

(*As Demea approaches the house the door opens and Micio appears.*)

MI. (*speaking to Aeschinus within.*) Ibo, íllis dicam núllam
    esse in nobís moram.
DE. (*aside.*) Sed ĕccum ípsum: (*aloud and angrily.*) te iam
    dúdum quaero, Mício.   720
MI. Quidnám? DE. Fero alia flágitia ad te ingéntia
Boni íllíus adulescéntis. MI. Ecce autém! DE. Nova,
Capitália. MI. (*impatiently.*) Ohe iam! DE. Néscis qui
    vir sít. MI. Scio.   5
DE. (*working himself into a passion.*) O stúlte, tu de psál-
    tria me sómnias
Agere: hóc peccatum in vírginem est civém. MI.
    (*quietly.*) Scio.   725
DE. Eho, scís et patere? MI. Quíd ni patiar? DE. Díc
    mihi,
Non clámas? non insánis? MI. Non: malím quidem—
DE. Puĕr nátust. MI. (*heartily with upraised hands.*) Di
    bene vórtant! DE. Virgo níl habet.   10
MI. Audívi. DE. Et ducenda índotata est. MI. Scílicet.
DE. Quid núnc futurum est? MI. Íd enim quod res ípsa
    fert: 730
Illínc huc (*pointing.*) transferétur virgo. DE. (*in a fury.*)
    O Iúppiter!
Istócine pacto opórtet? MI. Quid faciam ámplius?
DE. Quid fácias? si non ípsa re tibi ístúc dolet,   15
Simuláre certe est hóminis. MI. Quin iam vírginem
Despóndi: res compósita est: fiunt núptiae: 735

Dempsí metum omnem: haec mágĭs sunt hominis. **DE.**
    Céterum
Placét tibi factum, Mício? **MI.** Non, sí queam
Mutáre. nunc quom nón queo, animo aequó fero.   20
Ita víta est hominum, quási quom ludas tésseris,
Si illúd, quod maxume ópus est iactu, nón cadit,   740
Illúd quod cecidit fórte, id arte ut córrigas.
DE. (*sneeringly*.) Corréctor! nempe tua árte vigintí minae
Pro psáltria periére: quae quantúm potest   25
Aliquo ábicienda est, sí non pretio, grátiis.
MI. Neque ést, neque illam sáne studeo véndere.   745
DE. Quid ígitur facies? **MI.** Dómi erit. **DE.** (*in a tone
    of horror*.) Pro divóm fidem!
Psaltría ea et mater fámilias una ín domo?
MI. Quor nón? **DE.** Sanum te crédis esse? **MI.** Equi-
    dem árbitror.   30
DE. (*with angry sarcasm*.) Ita mé di ament, ut vídeo tuam
    ego inéptiam,
Factúrum credo, ut hábeas quicum cántites.   750
MI. Quor nón? **DE.** Et nova nupta éadem haec discet.
    MI. Scílicet.
DE. (*imitating the gestures of a dancer*.) Tu intér eas res-
    tim dúctans saltabís. **MI.** Probe.
DE. Probe? **MI.** (*seizing Demea by the hand and carica-
    turing his gestures*.) Ét tŭ nobiscum úna, si opŭs
    sit. **DE.** Heí mihi!   35
Non te haéc pudent? **MI.** Iam véro omitte, Démea,
Tuam ístanc iracúndiam, atque ita utí decet   755
Hilarum ác lubentem fác te gnati in núptiis.
Ego hós convenio: póst huc redeo. **DE.** (*exit into Sos-
    trata's house*.) O Iúppiter,
Hancíne vitam! hoscine móres! hanc deméntiam!   40

Vxór sine dote véniet: intus psáltria est:
Domŭs súmptuosa: aduléscens luxu pérditus: 760
Senéx delirans. ípsa si cupiát Salus,
Serváre prorsus nón potest hanc fámiliam.

SC. 8. [V. 1.]
SYRVS. DEMEA.

(*The door of Micio's house opens and Syrus reels on to the stage, intoxicated. He does not see Demea.*)
SY. (*in a tone of drunken satisfaction.*) Edepól, Syrisce,
    té curasti mólliter,
Lautéque munus ádministrastí tuom.
Abĭ. séd postquam intus sum ómnium rerúm satur, 765
Prodeámbulare huc lúbitum est. **DE.** Illud sís vide:
Exémplum disciplínae! **SY.** (*perceiving Demea.*) Ecce
    autem híc adest   •   5
Senĕx nóster. (*staggering towards Demea and addressing him familiarly.*) quid fit? quíd tu es tristis?
DE. (*angrily.*) Óh scelus!
SY. Ohe iám!· tu verba fúndis hic, sapiéntia?
DE. Tu sí meus esses—**SY.** (*with mock solemnity.*) Dís
    quidem esses, Démea, 770
Ac tuám rem constabilísses. (*giving a great lurch.*) **DE.**
    Exemplo ómnibus
Curárem ut esses. **SY.** (*in a tone of injured innocence.*)
    Quam ób rem? quid fecí? **DE.** (*furiously.*)
    · Rogas? 10
In ípsa turba atque ín peccato máxumo,
Quod víx sedatum sátis est, potastí, scelus,
Quasi ré bene gesta. **SY.** (*aside.*) Sáne nollem huc
    éxitum. 775

SC. 9. [V. 2.]
DROMO. SYRVS. DEMEA.

(*Dromo comes out of Micio's house and calls to Syrus.*)

DR. Heus Sýre, rogat te Ctésipho ut redeás. SY. (*apart to Dromo angrily as he pushes him off the stage.*) Abi.

DE. (*having only partly heard what Dromo said.*) Quid Ctésiphonem hic nárrat? SY. Nil. DE. Eho, cárnufex,

Est Ctésipho intus? SY. Nón est. DE. Quor hic nóminat?

SY. Est álius quidam, párasitaster paúlulus: Nostín? DE. (*going towards the door.*) Iam scibo. SY. (*catching hold of Demea's dress.*) Quíd agis? quŏ abis? DE. Mítte me.   5 780

SY. Noli ínquam. DE. Non manum ábstines, mastígia? (*pushing Syrus violently away, and shaking his stick at him.*)

An tíbi iam mavis cérebrum dispergam híc. (*dashes the door open and disappears into the house.*) SY. Abit.

Edepól commissatórem haud sane cómmodum,
Praesértim Ctesiphóni. quid ego núnc agam?
Nisi, dum haé silescunt túrbae, interea in ángulum   10 785
Aliquo ábeam atque edormíscam hoc villi. síc agam.
    (*exit reeling.*)

SC. 10. [V. 3.]

MICIO. DEMEA.

(*Micio comes out of Sostrata's house. Stopping at the door, he speaks to Sostrata within.*)

MI. Paráta a nobis súnt, ita ŭt dixi, Sóstrata,
Vbi vís. (*a loud knocking is heard within the door of his house.*) quisnam a me pépulit tam gravitér foris?
DE. (*bursting frantically from the house.*) Hei míhi! quid faciam? quíd agam? quid clamem aút querar?
O Caélum! O Terra! O Mária Neptuni! **MI.** (*aside.*)
    Ém tibi! 790
Rescívit omnem rem: íd nunc clamat: flicet, 5
Parátae lites; súccurrendum est. (*advances towards Demea.*)
    DE. Éccum adest
Commúnis corruptéla nostrum líberum.
MI. Tandém reprime iracúndiam atque ad té redi.
DE. (*restraining his anger with difficulty.*) Représsi, redii, mítto maledicta ómnia: 795
Rem ipsám putemus. dictum hoc inter nós fuit, 10
(Ex te ádeo est ortum), né tu curarés meum
Neve égo tuom? respónde. **MI.** Factum est, nón nego.
DE. Quor núnc apud te pótat? quor recipís meum?
Quor émis amicam, Mício? numquí minus 800
Mihi idém ius aequom est ésse quod mecúm est tibi? 15
Quando égo tuom non cúro, ne curá meum.
MI. Non aéquom dicis. **DE.** Nón? **MI.** Nam vetŭs verbum hóc quidem est,
Commúnia esse amícorum inter se ómnia.
DE. (*sarcastically.*) Facéte! nunc demum ístaec nata orátio est. 805

MI. (*quietly.*) Auscúlta paucis, nísi molestum est, Démea. 20
Princípio, si id te mórdet, sumptum fílii
Quem fáciunt, quaeso hoc fácito tecum cógites:
Tu illós duo olim pró re tollebás tua,
Quod sátĭs putabas túa bona ambobús fore,   810
Et mé tum uxorem crédidisti scílicet   25
Ductúrum: eandem illam rátionem antiquam óbtine:
Consérva, quaere, párce, fac quam plúrimum
Illís relinquas: glóriam tu istam óbtine. ·
Mea, quaé praeter spem evénere, utantúr sine.   815
De súmma nil decédet: quod hĭnc accésserit,   30
Id dé lucro putáto esse omne. haec sí voles
In ánimo vére cógitare, Démea,
Et mi ét tibi et illis démpseris moléstiam.
DE. Mittó rem: consuetúdinem ipsorúm—**MI.** (*interrupt-*
         ing.) Mane: 820
Scio: ístuc ibam. múlta in homine, Démea,   35
Signa ínsunt, ex quibŭs cóniectura fácile fit,
Duo quŏm idem faciunt, saépe ut possis dícere
'Hoc lícet inpune fácere huic, illi nón licet,'
Non quó dissimilis rés sit, sed quo is quí facit.   825
Quae ego inésse in illis vídeo, ut confidám fore   40
Ita ŭt vólumus. video eos sápere, intellegere, ín loco
Veréri, inter se amáre: scire est líberum
Ingénium atque animum. quóvis illos tú die
Reddúcas. at enim métuas, ne ab_re sínt tamen   830
Omíssiores paúlo. O noster Démea,   45
Ad ómnia alia aetáte sapimus réctius:
Solum únum hoc vitium adfért senectus hóminibus:
Atténtiores súmus ad rem omnes, quám sat est:
Quod íllós sat aetas ácuet. **DE.** (*sarcastically.*) Ne nimiúm
         modo   835

Bonaé tuae istae nós rationes, Mício, 50
Et túos iste animus aéquos subvortát. **MI.** Tace:
Non fíet. mitte iam ístaec: da te hodié mihi:
Expórge frontem. **DE.** (*with an ill grace.*) Scílicet ita
    témpus fert,
Faciúndum est: ceterúm rus cras cum fílio   840
Cum prímo luci ibo hínc. **MI.** De nocte cénseo: 55
Hodié modo hilarum fác te. **DE.** Et istam psáltriam
Vna flluc mecum hinc ábstraham. **MI.** (*clapping Demea
    on the shoulder.*) Pugnáveris.
Eo pácto prorsum illi ádligaris fílium.
Modo fácito ut illam sérves. **DE.** Ego ístuc vídero: 845
Atque íbi favillae pléna, fumi ac póllinis   60
Coquéndo sit faxo ét molendo: praéter haec
Merídie ipso fáciam ut stipulam cólligat;
Tam excóctam reddam atque átram quam carbo ést.
    MI. (*with a laugh.*) Placet:
Nunc míhi videre sápere: (*playfully caricaturing Demea's
    voice and action.*) atque equidem fílium   850
Tum etiám si nolit cógam ut illam sólam amet.   65
DE. (*bitterly.*) Derídes? fortunátu's, qui isto animó sies:
Ego séntio. **MI.** (*laying his hand affectionately on Demea's
    shoulder.*) Ah! pergísne? **DE.** Iam iam désino.
MI. I ergo íntro, et quoi rei est, eí rei hunc sumamús
    diem. (*exeunt into Micio's house.*)

ACTVS V.

SC. 1 [4].

DEMEA.

(*Demea comes out of Micio's house, having changed his coarse country dress for more fashionable attire.*)

Númquam ita quisquam béne subducta rátione ad vitám fuit, 855
Quín res, aetas, úsus, semper áliquid adportét novi,
Áliquid moneat: út illa quae te scísse credas néscias,
Ét quae tibi putáris prima, in éxperiundo ut répudies.
Quód nunc mi evenít: nam ego vitam dúram, quam vixi úsque adhuc, 5
Própe iam excurso spátio omitto. id quam ób rem? re ipsa répperi 860
Fácilitate nil esse homini mélius neque cleméntia.
Íd ësse verum ex me átque ex fratre quoívis facile est nóscere.
Ílle suam semper égit vitam in ótio, in convíviis,
Clémens, placidus, núlli laedere ós, adridere ómnibus: 10
Síbi vixit, sibi súmptum fecit: ómnes bene dicúnt, amant.
Égo ille agrestis, saévos, tristis, párcus, truculentús, tenax,
Dúxi uxorem: quam ibi miseriam vídi! nati fílii,
Ália cura: heia aútem! dum studeo illis ut quam plúrimum
Fácerem, contrivi ín quaerundo vítam atque aetatém meam: 15

Núnc exacta aetáte hoc fructi pró labore ab eís fero, 870
Ódium: ille alter síne labore pátria potítur cómmoda.
Íllum amant, me fúgitant: illi crédunt consilia ómnia,
Íllum diligúnt, apud illum súnt ambo, ego desértŭs sum:
Íllum ut vivat óptant, meam autem mórtem expectant
  scílicet.   20
Íta eos meo labóre eductos máxumo hic fecít suos 875
Paúlo sumptu: míseriam omnem ego cápio, hic potítur
  gaúdia.
Áge age, nunciam éxperiamur cóntra, ecquid ego póssiem
Bláa̲nde dicere aút benigne fácere, quando hoc próvocat.
Égo quoque a meís me amari et mágni fieri póstulo. 25
Si íd fit dando atque óbsequendo, nón posteriorés feram.
Déerit: id mea mínume refert, quí sum natu máxumus.

SC. 2 [5].

SYRVS. DEMEA.

(*Syrus appears at the door of Micio's house, and calls to Demea.*)
SY. Heus Démea! orat fráter ne abeas lóngius.
DE. Quis homo? (*with effusive politeness.*) Ó Syre noster,
  sálve! quid fit? quíd agitur?
SY. (*surprised.*) Recte. DE. Óptume est. (*aside.*) iam núnc
  haec tria primum áddidi   884
Praetér naturam: 'O nóster, quid fit? quíd agitur?'
(*to Syrus.*) Servom haúd inliberálem praebes te, ét tibi 5
Lubéns bene faxim. SY. (*bowing, but speaking in a tone
  of incredulous wonder.*) Grátiam habeo. DE.
  (*earnestly.*) Atquí, Syre,
Hoc vérum est, et re ipsa éxperiere própediem.

SC. 3 [6].

GETA. DEMEA. (SYRVS.)

(*Geta appears at the door of Sostrata's house.*)

GE. (*speaking to Sostrata within.*) Era, ego húc ad hos províso, quam mox vírginem
Arcéssant. (*turning round.*) sed ĕccum Démeam. salvós sies.   890
DE. (*affecting great interest.*) O quí vocare? **GE.** Géta.
    DE. Geta, hominem máxumi
Pretí te esse hodie iúdicavi animó meo:
Nam is míhi profecto est sérvos spectatús satis,   5
Quoi dóminus curae est, íta uti tibi sensí, Geta,
Et tíbi ob eam rem, síquid usus vénerit,   895
Lubéns bene faxim. (*aside.*) méditor esse adfábilis,
(*rubbing his hands with glee.*) Et béne prócedit. **GE.** Bónus es, quom haec exístumas.
DE. Paulátim plebem prímulum facio meam.   10

SC. 4 [7].

AESCHINVS. DEMEA. SYRVS. GETA.

(*Aeschinus comes on from Micio's house, not seeing Demea.*)

AE. (*wearily.*) Occídunt me equidem, dúm nimĭs sanctas núptias
Studĕnt fácere: in adparándo consumúnt diem.   900
DE. Quid ágitur, Aeschine? **AE.** Ehém! pater mi, tu híc eras?
DE. (*affectionately.*) Tuos hércle vero et ánimo et naturá pater,

Qui tĕ amat plus quam hosce óculos. sed quor nón do-
    mum 5
Vxórem arcessis? **AE.** (*with surprise.*) Cúpio: verum hoc
    míhi morae est,
Tibícina et hymenaéum qui cantént. **DE.** (*tapping Aes-
    chinus on the shoulder.*) Eho! 905
Vin tu huíc seni auscultáre? **AE.** Quid? **DE.** Missa haéc
    face,
Hymenaéum, turbas, lámpadas, tibícinas,
Atque hánc in hórto maceriam iubĕ dírui 10
Quantúm potest: hac tránsfer: unam fác domum:
Tradúce et matrem et fámiliam omnem ad nós. **AE.** (*de-
    lighted, embracing Demea.*) Placet, 910
Patér lepidissume! **DE.** (*aside.*) Eúge! iam lepidús vocor.
Fratri aédes fient pérviae, turbám domum
Addúcet, sumptu amíttet multa: quíd mea? 15
Ego lépidus ineo grátiam. (*aloud to Aeschinus.*) iubĕ
    núnciam
Dinúmeret ille Bábylo vigintí minas. 915
Syre, céssas ire ac fácere? **SY.** Quid ego? **DE.** Dírue.
    (*exit Syrus into Micio's house.*)
(*to Geta*). Tu illás abi et tradúce. **GE.** (*clasping his hands.*)
    Di tibi, Démea,
Bene fáciant, quom te vídeo nostrae fámiliae 20
Tam ex ánimo factum vélle. **DE.** Dignos árbitror. (*exit
    Geta, with a low bow, into Sostrata's house.*)
(*to Aeschinus.*) Quid tŭ aïs? **AE.** Sic opínor. **DE.** Multo
    réctiust 920
Quam illám puerperam hác nunc duci pér viam
Aegrótam. **AE.** Nil enim vídi melius, mí pater.
DE. (*in an off-hand tone*). Sic sóleo. (*the door of Micio's
    house opens.*) sed ĕccum Mício egréditúr foras. 25

SC. 5 [8].

MICIO. DEMEA. AESCHINVS.

(*Micio comes hastily from his house, speaking in a tone of incredulous amazement.*)

MI. Iubĕt fráter? ubi is est? tún iubes hoc, Démea?
DE. Ego véro iubeo et hác re et aliis ómnibus   925
Quam máxume unam fácere nos hanc fámiliam,
Colere, ádiuvare, adiúngere. **AE.** Ita quaesó, pater.
MI. (*astonished.*) Haud áliter censeo. **DE.** Ímmo hercle
    ita nobís decet: 5
Primum huíus uxori est máter. **MI.** Est. quid póstea?
DE. Proba ét modesta. **MI.** (*carelessly.*) Ita áiunt. **DE.**
    Natu grándior.   930
MI. (*emphatically.*) Scio. **DE.** Párere iam diu haéc per
    annos nón potest:
Nec qui eám respiciat quísquam est: sola est. **MI.** (*in
    wonder.*) Quam híc rem agit?
DE. Hanc te aéquom est ducere, (*turning to Aeschinus*)
    ét te operam ut fiát dare.   10
MI. (*in a tone of horror.*) Me dúcere autem? **DE.** Té.
    MI. Me? **DE.** Te inquam. **MI.** (*scornfully.*)
Inéptis. **DE.** (*to Aeschinus.*) Si tu sís homo,
Hic fáciat. **AE.** Mi patér! **MI.** (*angrily.*) Quid tu autem
    huic, ásine, auscultas? **DE.** Níl agis: 935
Fieri áliter non potést. **MI.** Deliras. **AE.** Síne te exo-
    rem, mí pater! (*laying his hand on Micio's
    shoulder.*)
MI. Insánis: (*angrily shaking off his son's hand.*) aufer!
    DE. (*laying his hand on Micio's other shoulder.*)

Áge, da veniam fílio. **MI.** (*shaking off Demea's hand.*) Satĭn sánus es?
Ego nóvŏs maritus ánno demum quínto et sexagé-
simo 15
Fiam, átque anum decrépitam ducam? idne éstis auc-
torés mihi?
AE. Fac: prómisi ego íllis. **MI.** (*sarcastically.*) Prómisti
autem? dé te largitór, puer. 940
DE. Age, quíd siquid te máius oret? **MI.** Quási non hoc
sit máxumum.
DE. (*again laying his hand on Micio's shoulder.*) Da véniam.
AE. (*laying his hand on Micio's other shoulder.*)
Ne gravére. **DE.** Fac, promítte. **MI.** (*in vain
trying to shake himself free.*) Non omíttitis?
AE. Non, nísi te exorem. **MI.** Vís est haec quidem.
DE. Áge, prolixe, Mícioǃ 20
MI. (*with a very ill grace.*) Etsi hóc mihi pravom, inép-
tum, absurdum, atque álienum a vitá mea
Vidétur: si vos tánto opere istuc vóltis, fiat. **AE.** Béne
facis. 945
Meritó te amo. **DE.** (*aside, in a meditative tone.*) Verúm
quid ego dicam, hóc quom confit quód volo?
Quid núnc quod restat? (*after a moment's pause, speaking
aloud to Micio.*) Hégio cognátus his est próxu-
mus,
Adfínis nobis, paúper: bene nos áliquid facere illí decet. 25
MI. Quid fácere? **DE.** Agelli est híc sub urbe paúlulŭm
quod locitás foras:
Huic démus qui fruátur. **MI.** Paululum id aútem est?
DE. Si multum ést, tamen 950
Faciúndum est: pro patre huíc est, bonus est, nóster
est, recté datur.

Postrémo non meum íllud verbum fácio, quod tu, Mício,
Bene ét sapienter díxti dudum? (*mimicking Micio's tones
 and gestures*) 'vítium commune ómnium est, 30
Quod nímium ad rem in senécta attenti súmus'? hanc
 maculam nós decet
Effúgere: dictum est vére et re ipsa fíeri oportet. **AE.**
 Mí pater! (*again laying his hand on Micio's
 shoulder.*) 955
MI. (*testily.*) Quid ístic? dabitur quándoquidem hic volt.
AE. Gaúdeo.
DE. Nunc míhi germanu's páriter animo et córpore.
(*aside, chuckling in great glee.*) Suó sibi gladio hunc
 iúgulo.

SC. 6 [9].

SYRVS. DEMEA. MICIO. AESCHINVS.

(*Syrus comes out of Micio's house, having pulled down part
 of the garden wall.*)

 SY. Factum est quód iussisti, Démea.
DE. Frúgi homo's. ergo édepol hodie meá quidem sen-
 téntia
Iúdico Syrŭm fíeri esse aequom líberum. **MI.** (*in a tone
 of indignant wonder.*) Istunc líberum? 960
Quódnam ob factum? **DE.** Múlta. **SY.** (*with insinuating
 address.*) O noster Démea, edepol vír bonu's:
Égo ístos vobis úsque a pueris cúravi ambos sédulo; 5
Dócui, monui, béne praecepi sémper quae potui ómnia.
DE. (*with jocular irony.*) Rés apparet: ét quidĕm porro
 haec, óbsonare cúm fide,

Psáltriam rapere, ádparare dé die convívium, 965
Nón mediocris hóminis haec sunt ófficia. **SY.** O lepidúm caput!
DE. Póstremo hodie in psáltria hac emúnda hic adiutór fuit, 10
Híc curavit: pródesse aequom est: álii meliorés erunt:
Dénique (*pointing to Aeschinus*) hic volt fíeri. **MI.** Vin tu hoc fíeri? **AE.** Cupio. **MI.** Sí quidem
Tú vis—(*beckoning to Syrus*) Syre, eho! accéde huc ad me: (*Micio performs the ceremony of manumission by turning Syrus round, and then letting him go with a box on the ear and the regular formula*) líber esto. **SY.** Béne facis: 970
Ómnibŭs gratiam hábeo, (*bowing to all in turn, but especially low to Demea,*) et seorsum tíbi praeterea, Démea.
DE. Gaúdeo. **AE.** Et ego. **SY.** Crédo: (*in a wheedling tone*) utinam hoc perpétuom fiat gaúdium, 15
Phrýgiam ut uxorém meam una mécum videam líberam.
DE. (*with effusion.*) Óptumam quidĕm múlierem. **SY.** Et quidĕm tuó nepoti, huius fílio,
Hódie prima mámmam dedit haec. **DE.** (*with mock solemnity.*) Hércle vero sério, 975
Síquidĕm prima dédit, haud dubium est quín emitti aequóm siet.
MI. Ób eam rem? **DE.** Ob eam: póstremo a me argéntum quanti est súmito. 20
SY. (*holding up his clasped hands to heaven.*) Dí tibi, Demea, ómnes semper ómnia optata ófferant!
MI. Sýre, processisti hódie pulchre. **DE.** Síquidĕm porro, Mício,

Tú tuom öfficium fácies, atque huic áliquid paulum praé
manu 980
Déderis, unde utátur, reddet tíbi cito. **MI.** (*snapping his
fingers.*) Istoc víIius.
AE. Frúgi homo est. **SY.** Reddam hércle, da modo.
AE. Áge, pater. **MI.** Post cónsulam. 25
DE. (*to Aeschinus.*) Fáciet. **SY.** O vir óptume! **AE.** O
patér mi festivíssume! ·
MI. (*to Demea.*) Quíd ïstuc? quae res tám repente móres
mutavít tuos?
Quód prolubium? quaé istaec subita est lárgitas? **DE.**
(*dropping his bantering air and speaking seriously.*)
Dicám tibi: 985
Vt id ostenderém, quod te isti fácilem et festivóm putant,
Íd non fieri ex véra vita, néque adeo ex aequo ét bono, 30
Séd ëx adsentando, índulgendo et lárgiendo, Mício.
(*turning to Aeschinus.*) Núnc adeo si ob eám rem vobis
méa vita invisa, Aéschine, est,
Quía non iusta iniústa, prorsus ómnia omnino óbse-
quor, 990
Míssa facio: effúndite, emite, fácite quod vobís lubet.
Séd si id voltis pótius, quae vos própter adulescéntiam 35
Mínŭs videtis, mágis inpense cúpitis, consulitís parum,
Haéc reprehendere ét corrigere et óbsecundare ín loco,
Ècce me, qui id fáciam vobis. **AE.** Tíbi, pater, per-
míttimus: 995
Plús scis quid facto ópus est. sed de frátre quid fiét?
DE. Sino:
Hábeat: in ïstac fínem faciat. **MI.** Ístuc recte. **CANTOR.**
(*advancing to the front of the stage.*) Plaúdite. 40

METRA HVIVS FABVLAE HAEC SVNT

Ver. 1 ad 154 iambici senarii
„ 155 ad 157 trochaici octonarii
„ 158 trochaicus dimeter catalecticus
„ 159 iambicus octonarius
„ 160 et 162 trochaici octonarii
„ 161, 163, 164 trochaici septenarii
„ 165 trochaicus octonarius
„ 166 iambicus octonarius
„ 167 ad 169 trochaici septenarii
„ 170 ad 196 iambici octonarii
„ 197 ad 208 trochaici septenarii
„ 209 iambicus septenarius
„ 210 ad 227 iambici octonarii
„ 228 ad 253 iambici senarii
„ 254 ad 287 iambici octonarii
„ 288 trochaicus septenarius
„ 289 ad 291 iambici octonarii
„ 292 et 293 trochaici septenarii
„ 294 iambicus octonarius
„ 295 ad 298 trochaici septenarii
„ 299 ad 302 iambici octonarii
„ 303 et 304 trochaici septenarii
„ 305 ad 316 iambici octonarii
„ 317 iambicus quaternarius
„ 318 et 319 trochaici septenarii
„ 320 iambicus octonarius
„ 321 ad 329 trochaici septenarii
„ 330 ad 354 iambici octonarii
„ 355 ad 516 iambici senarii
„ 517 trochaicus octonarius
„ 518 trochaicus septenarius
„ 519 ad 522 iambici octonarii

Ver. 523 trochaicus octonarius
„ 524 trochaicus dimeter catalecticus
„ 525 trochaicus octonarius
„ 526 trochaicus septenarius
„ 527 ad 539 iambici octonarii
„ 540 ad 591 trochaici septenarii
„ 592 ad 609 iambici octonarii
„ 610*a* iambicus monometer hypercatalecticus
„ 610*b* iambicus quaternarius
„ 611 iambicus octonarius
„ 612*a* trochaicus dimeter catalecticus
„ 612*b* iambicus dimeter catalecticus
„ 613 versus choriambicus
„ 614 iambicus senarius
„ 615 iambicus quaternarius
„ 616 trochaicus dimeter catalecticus
„ 617 trochaicus octonarius
„ 618 trochaicus septenarius
„ 619 ad 624 iambici octonarii
„ 625 ad 637 trochaici septenarii
„ 638 ad 678 iambici senarii
„ 679 ad 706 trochaici septenarii
„ 707 ad 711 iambici septenarii
„ 712 iambicus octonarius
„ 713 ad 854 iambici senarii
„ 855 ad 881 trochaici septenarii
„ 882 ad 933 iambici senarii
„ 934 ad 955 iambici octonarii
„ 956 et 957 iambici senarii
„ 958 ad 997 trochaici septenarii

NOTES.

NOTES.

Didascalia. The notices called *Didascaliae*, concerning the origin and first performance of Plautine and Terentian comedies, were inserted after the titles in the MSS. probably by grammarians of the Augustan age.

Adelphoe. This archaic form, corresponding to the Greek nom. pl. in -οι, is retained in the *Didascalia*, as also **Menandru** = Μενάνδρου.

The title is taken from one or both of the two pairs of brothers, Micio and Demea, Aeschinus and Ctesipho.

Graeca, i. e. *Comoedia palliata*, wherein the scene and characters are Greek, as opposed to a *Comoedia togata*, wherein they are Roman, or at any rate Italian. See Introduction xv.

funeralibus = *funebribus*: a form given by A here and in the *Didascalia* of the Hecyra: not found elsewhere.

L. Aemilio Paulo. This was the celebrated conqueror of Macedon, who was surnamed Macedonicus for his victory over Perseus at Pydna, B.C. 168. He died in B.C. 160. The Adelphi was performed for the first time, and the Hecyra for the second time, at these funeral games. Q. Fabius Maximus and P. Cornelius Scipio Africanus Minor were both his sons, who had been adopted, the former by the celebrated opponent of Hannibal, Q. Fabius Maximus Cunctator, the latter by the son of Africanus Major. According to D E F G they were curule aediles for the year, and so had official superintendence of the games.

egere, 'brought out.'

L. Ambivius Turpio was the manager who produced all Terence's plays. Cicero de Senect. 14. 48 mentions him as a good actor. With him is associated in all the *Didascaliae*, except that of the Hecyra, L. Atilius or Hatilius of Praeneste, of whom nothing further is known.

modos fecit, etc. 'The music by Flaccus, slave of Claudius, on Tyrian flutes throughout.' There seems to have been a sort of overture, and between the Acts lyrical monologues, called *Cantica*, were recited to a musical accompaniment. Sometimes, as in the Trinummus, a *Canticum* was embodied in the play itself. Cf. 610–6.

Claudi, sc. *servos*: he composed the music for all Terence's plays.

Sarranis. According to Servius *tibiae Sarranae* = *tibiae pares*, i.e. two of equal size and stops: *tibiae Phrygiae* = *tibiae impares*, i.e. two of unequal size and stops. Sarra was the old Latin for Tyre.

facta sexta, i. e. sixth in order of Terence's comedies.

Cethegus and **Gallus** were consuls 160 B. C.

ADELPHI.

Prologue.

It had been the custom of the earlier dramatists to give a plot of the Play in the Prologue : cf. 22. As dramatic art developed this was felt to be unnecessary, and Terence only followed the example set by Plautus in the Trinummus (if the Prologue of that play be authentic), in making the various characters of the comedy unfold its story to the audience. It was, however, an innovation either to write no Prologue at all—as at the first representation of the Hecyra, and possibly of the Andria—or to make the Prologue a vehicle for answering personal criticisms and attacking critics. The Prologue of the six plays of Terence are all genuine, while the twelve extant prologues of Plautus are all spurious, with the possible exception of that to the Trinummus.

1. **postquam** = *quoniam* (Donat.): contrast *quoniam* = *quom iam* Plaut. Aul. Prol. 9, the fact being that the ideas of sequence in time and of causality fade imperceptibly into each other.

poeta. Terence never introduces his own name, as Plautus sometimes does.

scriptura in Terence means (α) 'the work composed;' cf. Hec. Prol. 2. 13 *ne cum poeta scriptura evanesceret*; ib. 24.

(β) 'The style of the composition;' cf. Phor. Prol. 5 *fabulas tenui esse oratione et scriptura levi*. The former sense is here preferable.

Notice the double alliteration, which however Terence does not use to the same extent as Plautus, though examples are frequent in his prologues. Cf. 3, 7, 11, 13, 19, 21. Jordan calculates that an alliteration occurs in about every 9 lines of Plautus and 20 lines of Terence.

2. **iniquis**, sc. Luscius Lanuvinus and his party; cf. Andr. 7, Phor. 1 and 13, Haut. 22.

observari = *captari* (Donat.), 'criticised.'

3. **rapere in peiorem partem**, 'pick to pieces.'

quam, sc. *fabulam*.

4. The text gives the MSS. reading. To avoid *erit* some editors omit *eritis* and read *sese*.

indicio erit = *index erit*, 'he will give evidence about himself.'

5. **id factum**, sc. the introduction of a scene from one play into another, as he proceeds to explain. This plan of amalgamating parts of two plays into one, technically termed *contaminare*, was made a special point of attack by his 'malevolent' critics. Terence acknowledges and defends his practice here, and in the Prologues to the Andria (13–21), Eunuchus (31–34), and Hauton Timorumenos (16–19).

NOTES. LINES 1–23.

6. Diphili. Diphilus of Sinope was a writer of the New Attic comedy, contemporary with Menander. The Rudens and Casina of Plautus were adapted from his plays.

7. Commorientis. This play has been entirely lost.

9. in prima fabula, 'in the early part of the play.'

10. integrum, 'untouched,' its original meaning.

eum, monosyllabic by synizesis and then elided. See Introduction.

hic, sc. Terence; cf. 18. There is no other instance of 'contamination' known, where the originals were taken from different poets.

11. verbum de verbo expressum, 'translated word for word.' This is meant to commend the play to 'the public;' cf. Introduction xiv and xvi.

extulit = *transtulit*, probably for the sake of alliteration.

13. furtum. Cf. Eun. 23.

factum, sc. *esse*. Terence very frequently omits some part of *esse* in passive tenses, e.g. 14.

15. nam quod isti dicunt malevoli, 'for as to the assertion of those spiteful people.'

isti, 'those of the opposite party.' Cf. 43.

malevoli, a favourite epithet for Luscius Lanuvinus and other critics. Cf. Andr. 6, Haut. 16 and 22.

homines nobiles, i.e. the members of the Scipionic circle. See Introduction xiv.

18. eam for *id* by attraction.

hic. Cf. 10.

quom. This was the correct spelling in early Latin. Cicero wrote *cum*: *quum* is post-Augustan. In the republican period *u* was replaced by *o* after another *u* or *v*. Such forms as *ingenuus, servus*, etc. were not written until the latter part of the first century A.D.

19. vobis univorsis, 'all of you,' i.e. the audience.

populo, 'the public,' i.e. the Roman people generally.

20. in otio, 'at leisure,' especially for literary pursuits, opposed to both *in bello* and *in negotio*.

21. Translate, 'no one disdains to use at his own convenience.' The argument is, 'no one is too proud to avail himself of the services of these great men in other matters; why should I in composing my plays?' To connect *sine superbia* with *homines nobiles* is not only opposed to the collocation of the words, but also to the sense.

22. dehinc, always monosyllabic in Terence.

23. ii, the reading of A with D G P. Most editors, following

Ritschl on Pl. Trin. 17 (Prolegomena 98), print *i* or *ci*. Priscian says that *ii* was pronounced as one syllable. Lines 22-3 are almost verbally identical with Pl. Trin. 16-7.

24. **ostendent**, sc. *actores*. Terence not unfrequently leaves a subject to be supplied, when the sense is obvious, especially if the verb be in the infinitive, e.g. 52. Cf. 77 note.

aequanimitas, 'your kind attention:' cf. Andr. 24, Haut. 35, Phor. 30 *adeste aequo animo*.

25. **augeat**. Ritschl (Proleg. 180-3) shows that the singular terminations of the pres. subj. act. and the 1st pers. sing. of pres. subj. pass. or deponent may be lengthened, when the accent falls upon them.

ACT I. SCENE 1.

Micio calls for Storax, one of the slaves sent the night before to escort his adopted son Aeschinus home from supper. Receiving no answer, he supposes that they have not returned, and proceeds to moralise on the anxieties of a parent and the best system of education.

27. **servolorum**, etc. Donatus tells us that slaves to whom this duty was assigned were called *advorsitores*. The diminutive *servoli* is used in a similar connexion Andr. 83. Cf. 566.

ierant, as Phor. 573 *audīeras*, Hec. 813 *audīerit*, but 127 *ablero*. So Terence uses *fierem* and *fierem*.

29-30. Ritschl considers *aut ibi si cesses* and *et quae in animo cogitat* as spurious, and reads but one line,

quae in te uxor dicit, evenire ea satius est.

All MSS. however have the words, and there is some point in the idea of the angry wife who says something, but thinks a good deal more.

ibi, sc. *uspiam*.

in te rather than *de te*, expressing the spiteful intent of the words.

31. **propitii**, 'loving:' more commonly used of deities.

33. **animo obsequi**, 'to make merry,' lit. 'to follow one's inclinations:' cf. Pl. Mil. Gl. 677 *es, bibe, animo obsequere mecum, atque onera te hilaritudine*. Similar phrases are *animum explere, animo morem gerere*; cf. Andr. 188, 641.

34. **soli**, 'left all alone:' this seems better than to connect *soli* with *tibi*. The line is wanting in A.

35. **ĕgŏ quĭă**, a proceleusmatic. See Introduction xxvi.

37-8. The text gives the MSS. reading. Fleckeisen follows Ritschl's conjectural emendation (Proleg. 120),

Aut ceciderit aliqua atque aliquid praefregerit.
Vah! quemquamne hominem in animum instituere aut sibi ...

quemquamne, etc. Terence often uses the acc. and inf. to express indignant or excited questions and exclamations: 'to think that any man ...'

-ne is frequently found in such sentences, because a question is implied if not expressed: cf. 304 note, 237, 330, 390, 408, 449, 562, 610, 629.

in animum instituere, 'should take it into his head.'

39. **parare** is dependent on *in animum instituere*.

40. **atque**, 'and yet.' This adversative sense is not uncommon in Terence, e.g. 362, Andr. 225, etc.

The text gives the reading of all the MSS. except A, which has *ex fratre meo is dissimili ...*, but *meo* is an alteration by a later hand and *is dissimili* cannot be kept. Donatus reads *is adeo*.

41. **iam inde ab adulescentia.** Cf. 962 *usque a pueris*.

42. **clementem**, 'easy-going.'

43. **quod**, sc. *uxorem non habere*.

isti, 'those who are not like me,' 'my married friends.' This is better than to understand *quod* = *uxorem habere*, and *isti*, as 'those who differ from me.'

44. **contra.** Many editors, believing that *contra* is not used as a preposition as early as Terence, put a stop after *omnia*, and suppose an ellipse of *agit* or some such word. But, though the adverbial use is much more common, e. g. 50, *contra* is found as an undoubted preposition Pl. Ps. 155 *adsistite omnes contra me*, ib. Pers. 1. 1. 13, and it is far more natural to take it as such here and in the parallel passage, Phor. 521 *nunc contra omnia haec Repperi qui det neque lacrumet*.

45. **agere**, historic infinitive, a marked characteristic of Terence's style. Here he even uses *agere* and *habere* as coordinate with *duxit*.

47. **inde** = *ex eis*.

hunc, sc. Aeschinus.

48. **eduxi** = *educavi*, as often in old Latin. Cf. 495, 875.

49. **in eo**, 'therein,' i. e. in my care and love for Aeschinus.

50. **contra**, 'in return,' an adverb. Cf. 44 note.

me, sub. *carum*.

51. **do** *sumptum* ; **praetermitto** *delicta* (Don.).

52. **pro meo iure**, 'by my authority.'

agere. The subject is *eum*, understood. Cf. 24 note.

clanculum, ἅπαξ λεγόμενον as a preposition with acc., elsewhere an adverb. It is a diminutive from *clam*.

53. **fert**, 'is prone to,' lit. 'brings one to.' Contrast 730 note.

55. insuerit=*insueverit*, also used transitively.

56. The MSS. read
aut audebit tanto magis audebit ceteros.
Several emendations are proposed:
audebit tanto magis audacter ceteros.
[Speng. Pless.]
audacter tanto magis audebit ceteros.
[Dzi.]
The text follows Ritschl.

57-8. 'To keep one's hold on the children of gentlemen by honour and gentlemanly feeling.'

liberi are freeborn children as opposed to *servi.* Cf. 449, 684, 828.

The juxtaposition of two words of the same root is common in Terence, e. g. 20, 211-12, 322, 384, 668, 990. This is merely a special form of *assonance*, and is to be distinguished from *agnominatio* or *paronomasia*, which, strictly speaking, is a play upon words of similar sound but different sense, something akin to a pun, e. g. Andr. 218 *inceptio est amentium, haud amantium.* Paronomasia is fairly common in Plautus, but rare in Terence. The term is sometimes extended to a play upon different meanings of the same word, such as is not uncommon in Cicero.

59. conveniunt. In this sense *convenire* is usually impersonal, or in the phrase *res convenit.*

60. All MSS. read *clamitans, quid agis Micio?* It is a less violent change to read *clamans*, than with Wagner and Plessis to omit *agis*.

61. quor=*cur*, from *qua re.*

nobis, an ethic dative. Cf. 276, 476.

63. vestitu=*vestitui*, dative. This form is found in Lucretius, Sallust, Vergil, etc., and is said by Gellius to have been always used by Caesar; cf. Verg. A. 1. 257 *parce metu, Cytherea,* Haut. 357 *neglectu.*

64. aequomque et bonum. *Polysyndeton*, or redundance of copulas, is not uncommon in Terence, e. g. Andr. 676 *noctisque et dies;* cf. 301. Livy and Sallust, whose style presents many points of similarity with that of Terence, write -*que et* not unfrequently.

68. ratio, 'system.'

69. malo, 'by punishment;' often in this sense, e. g. Andr. 179, 431, etc.

70. id, *quod facit scilicet* (Don.). All MSS. but A and G read *cavet.*

71. fore clam, 'that it will be kept secret;' a peculiar use of *clam*.

ad ingenium, 'to his natural bent.'

72. The second foot may be a proceleusmatic or a tribrach, in which latter case -*io* of *beneficio* must be considered as one syllable by Synizesis and elided. Cf. 79, 254.

ex animo, 'sincerely;' often so used in Terence, e.g. 919.

74. patrium, 'a father's duty.' Strictly *patrius* is what refers to the nature of a father, *paternus* what comes from the father, as property, etc. Cf. 450, 871.

75. alieno = *aliorum*.

76. hoc, ablative, 'herein.'

hoc qui nequit, sc. *facere*. One other instance, Pl. Merc. 3. 4. 51, is sometimes quoted of *nequeo* with a direct object; but it is better to consider both passages as elliptical.

77. For the omission of the subject *se* cf. 24. Cf. 151, 162, 193, 270, 359, 401, 402, 415, 429, 750, 826. A similar omission is common in Livy, and in most poets.

79. nescio quid tristem, 'somewhat out of temper;' cf. 866. *Nescio quid* is often thus used to qualify an adjective or verb; cf. 211. *Nescio* may be scanned as a dactyl, or as a spondee by Synizesis of *-io*; cf. 72.

credo, parenthetical, as often in Terence, e.g. 226, 339, 411.

80. iurgabit, 'he will scold.' Cf. Cic. Rep. 4. 8. 4 *iurgare lex putat inter se vicinos, non litigare*.

Act I. Scene 2.

Demea has heard that Aeschinus has forcibly carried off a music-girl from her master's house. Considering that Micio's indulgence is the root of the evil, he comes to reproach him bitterly. Micio turns the tables upon his brother, and after a stormy scene reduces him to a sullen silence. After Demea's departure Micio gives expression to his anxiety about Aeschinus.

81. Plautus never begins a scene with a broken line, as Terence does here and elsewhere, e.g. 635, 958.

quaerito, 'I am anxious to find.' Note the intensive force of the frequentative verb. Cf. 321, 363.

82-3. ubi nobis Aeschinus siet, 'since we have an Aeschinus.' For *ubi* in this sense and construction cf. Pl. Amph. 439 *ubi ego Sosia esse nolim, tu esto sane Sosia*. The text gives the reading of all MSS. Many editors adopt Ritschl's conjecture:

DE. *Rogas me? ubi nobis Aeschinust?*
Scin iam quid tristis ego sim?

siet, archaic for *sit*. Terence uses *siem* e.g. 712, *sies* e.g. 684, 852, 890, *siet* e.g. 282, 298, 611, 976, *sient*; also *possiem* 877, *adsiet* 619.

dixin hoc fore? 'did I not say this would be so?' Some editors, against the MSS., give these words to Demea.

-ne = *nonne*, as often in Terence and Plautus. Indeed, it is doubtful whether *nonne* was found in the original MSS. of these writers, *-ne* or *non* being used indifferently. Cf. 94 note, 727, etc.

84. **quid ille fecerit?** The subj. depends on the ellipse of *rogas*, or some similar word. It is common in an indignant or excited repetition of a question asked by another, e.g. 261, 374.

pudet, occasionally personal in Plautus and Terence, the subject being usually a pronoun. Cf. 754.

86. **antehac.** See Introduction on Prosody xxix.

87. **modo quid designavit?** 'what new outrage has he perpetrated?' *modo* = 'just now.' *designare* in a bad sense is rare.

89. **familiam**, i.e. the slaves. Cf. 297 note.

90. **usque ad mortem**, 'almost to death.' Notice this sense of *usque ad*, 'right up to, but just stopping short of.' Cf. Andr. 199.

92. **quot.** All MSS. here read *quod*, but A regularly gives *quod* and *aliquod* for *quot* and *aliquot*.

94. **non** = *nonne*. Cf. 83 note, 754, 781, 942, 952.

95. **rei dare operam**, 'looking after the property.' The infinitive construction after *videre*, in place of a participle, is not common.

96. **huius**, gen. neut., sc. this conduct of Aeschinus (cf. 92 *hoc*), dependent on *simile*, which always governs a gen. in Plautus and Terence. Cf. 411. It is possible, however, to understand *huius* of Ctesipho as a gen. after *factum*.

illi, dat. incommodi.

98. **inperito**, 'with no experience of life.'

numquam, used as an emphatic negative: cf. 528, 551, etc.

100. **quorsum istuc?** sc. *pertinet aut dicis* (Don.), 'what do you mean by that?'

101. **flagitium**, a much stronger word than *peccatum*, 'there is nothing shameful.'

104. **siit** = *sivit*, on the authority of A. The contracted perf. is found several times in Plautus, e.g. Trin. 520-1 *ne tu illunc agrum Tuom siris umquam fieri*, Mil. Gl. 1072 *sisti*.

106. **esset... fieret... faceremus.** This use of the imperf. subj. for the pluperf. subj. is an idiom often found in the best authors; sometimes even the pres. subj. is substituted for an imperf. or pluperf. Cf. Madvig, Lat. Gr. § 347, obs. 1-3; infra 178.

fieret. The first syllable of *fieri*, *fierem*, etc. is usually long in Plautus and Terence. Cf. 27 note.

107. **si esses homo**, 'if you had the feelings of a man.' Cf. 734, 736, 934; also 579 for a different shade of meaning.

109. **ubi te... foras**, 'after tumbling you out of doors, a corpse

long waited for;' *eicere* is a brutal substitute for *efferre*. The phrase purposely suggests more than it expresses. Cf. 874.

110. **alieniore**, 'less suitable.'

foras, an acc. pl. of the obsolete *fora*, used as an adverb meaning 'motion out of doors;' so *foris*, abl. pl., means 'rest out of doors.' For the position of tamen cf. 174, 226.

116. **illi**, 'therein,' archaic form of *illic*, often found in Plautus, sometimes in Terence, and perhaps in Vergil G. 1. 54, 251, 3. 17. Cf. 577, 844. *illi* might, however, be here considered as a dative.

117. **de meo**, sc. *patrimonio*, 'the expense is mine.' Cf. 940, Pl. Trin. 328.

123. **cĕdŏ**. This archaic imperative is used by Cicero. The plural form *cette* is only found in old Latin. Cf. 688.

124. **ei**, interjection, also written *hei*.

127. **consulis**. So BCDFGPV, E *consilis*, A *consiliis*. The reading in the text seems to have been the only one known to Donatus; it is intrinsically preferable, and the mistake of copying *consiliis* from the line before so probable, that we have followed Fleckeisen, Wagner, and Plessis in printing *consulis*. For the assonance cf. 57 note.

si pergis, abĭero, 'if you are going on so, I will be off.' A future perfect is often used by Plautus and Terence to express a future action to be quickly and certainly performed, where in English we should employ a future simple. Cf. 209, 538, 819, 845. On the quantity of *abĭero* see 27 note.

128. **sicine agis?** 'what, act thus?' i.e. go away without another word.

129. **curae est mihi**, sc. *ea res*. Cf. 128.

133. **quid istic**, 'well then,' a formula of assent, usually reluctant or impatient, after discussion; cf. 350, 956. The phrase is elliptical: cf. Pl. Ep. 1. 2. 38 *quid istic verba facimus*. *Istic* is an adverb.

134. Notice the alliteration. Cf. 1 note.

135. **unum**. Some MSS. read *ullum*. For *aposiopesis* cf. 137.

136. **an non credis?** The sentence, like all those wherein *an* introduces a question, is elliptical, the first member of a disjunctive sentence being suppressed. The full phrase would be *Mihin credis an non*? Translate, 'Do not you believe me?'

repeto, so A, omitting the interrogative particle, as is common in conversation, where the question is asked by the tone of the voice. Cf. 619, 641, 737.

137. **aegre est**, ''tis very hard.'

139. **quom...est**, 'since he (Ctesipho) is...' In Plautus often, in Terence occasionally, *quom* causal is found with the indicative. Cicero also uses this construction after such verbs as *laudo, gaudeo, doleo, gratulor*. Cf. 738, 897, 918, Andr. 488, 623, 771, Phor. 208.

sentiet, sc. how much better off his sober brother is.

141. **nec nil neque omnia,** 'neither groundless nor altogether right.'

142. **haec,** sc. the conduct of Aeschinus.

143. **aegre pati.** Cf. Andr. 137 *aegre ferens*.

homo, sc. Demea.

144. **quom placo ... deterreo,** 'when I want to quiet him, I contradict him flatly and out-face him.'

145. **vix humane patitur,** 'he scarcely takes it reasonably;' *humane* lit. 'as a man should.'

augeam, sc. *iracundiam*.

151. **dixit velle.** Cf. 77 note.

152. **defervisse,** 'had cooled down;' *de* in composition, like ἀπό, often means 'to come to an end,' 'to cease.' Cf. Verg. A. 4. 52 *dum pelago desaevit hiems*.

153. **nisi,** 'yet.' This adversative sense of *nisi* is found in a few other passages, e.g. Eun. 547 *nequeo satis mirari neque conicere ; Nisi, quidquid est, procul hinc lubet prius quid sit sciscitari* : ib. 997.

154. **hominem,** sc. Aeschinus.

ACT II. SCENE I.

Aeschinus, after breaking into Sannio's house, carries off the music-girl, with whom Ctesipho is in love. Sannio endeavours to prevent her being taken into Micio's house, but only gets soundly cuffed for his pains, and is left outside to recount his grievances to the audience.

This is the scene taken from the Synapothnescontes of Diphilus, mentioned in the Prologue, 6-11. The 'contamination' accounts for certain discrepancies of detail, e.g. Demea, v. 93, spoke of the outrage as already of public notoriety, whereas here it is represented as having only just occurred. Again, in 355-6, Demea has heard that Ctesipho had a hand in the abduction of the girl, but there is no hint of this elsewhere: indeed, the contrary is distinctly implied by Ctesipho himself in Act II. Sc. 3.

Moreover, in the original the music-girl probably proved to be an Athenian citizen, as she is called by Aeschinus in 194; and this would explain the open violence of his proceedings. For had Sannio detained as a slave a free-born Athenian, he would be liable to severe penalties, and Aeschinus might without risk attempt to drag him forcibly before the courts. Otherwise he would scarcely have turned Sannio out of his house, and maltreated him in the public street (198). But that Terence

NOTES. LINES 141–166.

did not intend to represent the girl as free-born is plain from the fact that so important a point is never again alluded to, either by Sannio in his soliloquy or by Syrus in the following scene.

155. Notice the change to trochaic metre, expressive of strong excitement.

156. nunciam = *nunc iam*. See Introduction on Prosody xxix.

ilico (*in-loco*) is occasionally used in early Latin in its original sense of *place*, not as later of *time*. There is no other certain instance in Terence, as Phor. 195 *sta ilico* could be taken either way; but see Pl. Bacch. 1140 *ilico ambae manete*.

hic, i.e. before Micio's door.

157. hic, i.e. Sannio.

158. istam, sc. *tangam*.

159. non committet ... vapulet, 'he will not expose himself to a second thrashing to-day.' Cf. Pl. Trin. 704.

160. meorum morum, 'of my character.' Note the alliteration and assonance. Cf. 1 and 57 notes. *Meorum* and *fuisse* are dissyllabic by Synizesis.

161. Sannio's meaning has been sometimes mistaken. What he is appealing to, as a plea for consideration from Aeschinus, is not his position as slave-dealer, which, though protected by law, was held in the most utter contempt (cf. Pl. Rud. 651–3), but his excellent character (*mores*), which would secure him justice before a court. The sense is, 'I am a slave-dealer, it is true, but no man living ever bore a better character.'

fide optuma, abl. of quality constructed with *quisquam*, which is used because the sentence is virtually negative.

162. tu quod ... purges, 'and as to the excuse you may make afterwards.' Cf. Andr. 395 *nam quod tu speres*, '*propulsabo facile uxorem ...*'

purges is a potential subjunctive, that is, the apodosis of a conditional sentence, the protasis of which is suppressed.

quod is an acc. of respect. Cf. Zumpt, Lat. Gr. § 627. Cf. 296, 299, 305, 835.

163. huius, elliptical gen. of price: δεικτικῶς. Cf. 278.

faciam, fut. ind.

165–6. The text gives the reading of A F P. This makes 165 a trochaic tetrameter, and 166 an iambic tetrameter. This change of metres is so unusual that many editors have transposed or altered words to avoid it. But it should be noted that the metre changes from trochaic tetrameters, 155–7, followed by one trochaic dimeter catalectic, v. 158, to an iambic tetrameter in 159; and in both cases the change coincides with the actual or imputed words of Aeschinus, contrasted in their measured tones with the excited utterance of Sannio.

nollem factum, sc. *esse*, a form of apology. Cf. 162, 775, 919.

indignum... indignis. There is a play upon the meanings 'undeserving' and 'undeserved,' 'shameful.'

acceptus, 'treated.' Cf. Pl. Aul. 4. 4. 3.

167. **abi prae.** Cf. Andr. 171 *i prae*.

hoc, i.e. 'these expostulations.'

nihili facis. Cf. 163.

168. **nunciam.** Cf. 156 note. Most MSS. read *I intro nunciam tu. Sa. At enim...* A omits both *tu* and *at*, one of which is necessary for the metre.

at enim, 'but indeed.' Plautus and Terence often use *enim* or *nam* with an intensive force, emphasising the word before or after it. Cf. 656, 721, 730, 788, 830, 922. In Pl. Trin. 1134 *enim* with this meaning begins a sentence.

169. **propter hunc**, 'close by him.' Cf. 576. Cicero and Vergil also use *propter* in a local sense.

em = *en* frequently in the MSS. of the comic poets; probably to be distinguished from *hem*, but the MSS. vary greatly, and it is often difficult to decide between them. Cf. 537, 559.

172. **ergo** is often used as an emphasising particle, especially in questions or imperative phrases. Cf. 324, 326, 572. 'I very much wish he would try that game on.'

hem! serva, 'hah! look out.' The same phrase occurs Andr. 416.

173. The text gives the MS. reading. In the scansion *cavēs* may be shortened (see Introduction), or else pronounced as a monosyllable, as seems to have been the case from the story told by Cicero de Div. 2. 40. 84, where the huckster's cry '*Cauneas*' (*ficus*) is represented as identical in sound with *cave ne eas*. Ritschl, Proleg. 151–152, gives numerous instances of a similar character.

174. **peccato...**, 'err on that side rather than on the other.' The so-called future imperative (used in laws, etc.) has a comical appropriateness here, as if Aeschinus were laying down a general rule of conduct.

tamen. Cf. 110.

175. **regnumne.** Cf. Phor. 405 *quandoquidem solus regnas et soli licet*, Pl. Trin. 695 *quid? te dictatorem censes fore...?* This can hardly be considered as a distinctively Roman allusion, as a 'tyrant' was almost as great a bug-bear at Athens as a 'king' was at Rome.

hic, sc. at Athens.

176. **ornatus... virtutibus.** Aeschinus is of course speaking

ironically, perhaps with reference to 161. Plautus Capt. 997 uses the same phrase: *ornatus*, 'dressed.'

177. 'What business have you with me?'

178. **ferres.** Cf. 106 note.

179. **qui**, 'how,' an old form of the ablative, used by Plautus and Terence in several senses:

(1) As a relative, referring to any gender and either number. Cf. 254, 477, 750.

(2) As a final particle, with the subjunctive—'in order that.' Cf. 950.

(3) As an interrogative adverb—'how.' Cf. the present passage, 215, 891.

(4) As an indefinite particle with words of emphasis—'somehow' (Gr. πώs), e.g. *hercle qui, edepol qui, quippe qui, et qui*. Cf. 800 *numqui*.

(5) Introducing curses (πῶs, *utinam*),—'would that,' 'O that.' Cf. Phor. 123, Pl. Trin. 923, 997.

It is commonly used by later writers in *atqui, alioqui*, etc., and rarely in one or other of the above senses.

magis, i.e. rather than for me to have your property.

181. **abripiere.** Plautus and Terence usually employ the form in *-re* of second pers. sing. pass. in preference to that in *-ris*, except for metrical reasons. Cicero follows the same custom except in the pres. ind. and Vergil also. On the other hand Livy and Tacitus seldom use the form in *-re*.

182. **loris liber.** Only slaves could legally be scourged.

For alliteration cf. 1 note.

183. **O hominem.** For the hiatus see Introduction. Cf. 304, 336.

184. **debacchatus es.** The verb is only found elsewhere Hor. Od. 3. 3. 55.

185. **autem** is used as an emphatic particle, especially with pronouns. Cf. 404, 537, 934, 935, 940, 950, Verg. A. 2. 101.

187. **aequi modo aliquid**, sc. *dicas*, 'provided you say something fair.'

190. **etiam hoc restat.** Cf. 357.

191. **minis viginti**, i.e. about £80. The usual price of female slaves in these comedies is twenty or thirty minae, sometimes more.

192. **ĕgŏ tĭbi ĭllam.** Notice the proceleusmatic, formed, as usual, of two distinct pairs of short syllables.

193. **vendundam**, sc. *esse*. This was the archaic form of the gerundive. At the period of Terence the forms in *-undus* and *-endus* were used side by side for verbs of the third or fourth conjugation, except that *-undus* is never admitted where the verb-stem ends in *u* or *v*. The older form was much affected by Sallust, and is frequently found in

Augustan writers, especially in legal or political phrases (e. g. *iure dicundo, res repetundae*), being most common in verbs of the fourth conjugation: *ire* and its compounds always retain the form in *-undus*, while *gerundus* and *ferundus* are usually found in Cicero, Caesar, and Livy. The older form is, however, seldom used for the gerund.

194. **quae libera est.** See note at beginning of this scene.

nam ego ... manu, 'for I f rmally maintain her freedom by legal process.' Aeschinus uses legal phrases: *adserere manu* = to declare a person free by the symbolical action of laying one's hand on him: *causa liberalis* = an action to recover liberty. Cf. Gr. ἀφαίρεσις εἰς ἐλευθερίαν.

195. **vide utrum vis.** Note the indicative. Cf. 228-229, 342, 513, 559, 630, 996. 'In conversational or animated language a question is often put, logically though not grammatically dependent on another verb or sentence, e.g. on such expletives as *dic mihi, loquere, cedo, responde, expedi, narra, vide; rogo, volo scire, fac sciam, viden, audin, scin*, etc. So frequently in Plautus and Terence, even where later writers would make the question dependent and use the subjunctive.' Compare English, 'Tell me, where are you?' 'Tell me where you are?' Roby, School Lat. Gr. § 751.

causam meditari, 'to get up your case.'

196. **dum,** 'until,' is often found, even in Cicero, with a pres. ind. when the future action is represented as certain, especially after verbs of 'waiting.' Cf. 785, Andr. 329 *profer (nuptias) dum proficiscor*, ib. 714, Phor. 982.

198. **domo me eripuit.** See note at beginning of this scene.

199. **plus** (*minus* and *amplius* also), when joined to numerals, is used with or without *quam*, and without influence on the construction.

infregit = *illisit, inflixit* (Don.).

All MSS. place line 200 of this edition before line 199. All editors agree in the transposition.

200. **tantidem ... tradier,** 'to be handed over to him at cost price.' The archaic form in *-ier* of the pres. inf. pass. is often used by poets. The final *-er* is probably the sign of the passive, but the history of its origin and change into the later form is quite uncertain. Cf. 273, 535, 607.

202. **hariolor,** 'I am talking nonsense.' Cf. Phor. 492. The significant change in the meaning of this verb shows pretty clearly into what disrepute soothsaying must have fallen before this date. So μαίνομαι and μαντική are connected. Cf. Plato Phaedr. 245 B, C.

203. **ubi me dixero dare** = *ubi dixero me daturum esse mulierem Aeschino*. Terence not unfrequently uses the pres. inf. after verbs of promising, saying, etc., where we should expect the fut. inf. The same

construction is occasionally found in prose writers of the Augustan age. E. g. Caesar B. G. 4. 21 *pollicentur obsides dare*. The present tense has really a continuative force, which in certain connexions makes it almost equivalent to a future. Cf. 224.

204. Sannio means that, if he agrees to sell the girl, he will not be able to prosecute Aeschinus for her violent abduction, while his chance of getting the purchase-money will be remote.

somnium, 'moon-shine.' Cf. 395.

205. **id**, sc. the delay.

206. **eum quaestum**, 'that business,' i.e. of slave-dealing.

inceperis, so all MSS. Many editors *occeperis*.

208. **has rationes puto**, 'I make these calculations.' Cf. 796 note.

Act II. Scene 2.

Aeschinus, knowing that he might fare ill were Sannio to prosecute him, sends out Syrus, a crafty slave, to arrange matters. Owing to complications in his affairs Sannio cannot afford to delay for a law-suit, and begs Syrus to use his good offices to obtain for him the cost-price of the music-girl.

209. **conveniam ipsum.** A gives CONVENIAMIAMIPSUM.

This insertion of *iam* is a good instance of *dittography*, i. e. a repetition through an error of the copyist of the same or similar letters, a fruitful source of corruption in MSS. Thus many MSS. insert *iam* after *accipiat* in this line, which is almost certainly a mistake of the same character.

faxo. Plautus and Terence use the following, *faxo* (ind.), *faxim* (subj.), *faxis, faxit* (ind. or subj.), *faxīmus* (subj.), *faxitis* (ind. or subj.), *faxint* (subj.). Two views are held with regard to these forms:

(1) They may be syncopated forms for *fecero, fecerim*, etc.: cf. Zumpt, § 161.

(2) They may be archaic futures, formed exactly like the Greek by adding *-so* to the verb-stem, e. g. *fac-so* = *faxo* as πραγ-σω = πράξω: the tense in *-sim* being the subjunctive: cf. Roby, §§ 291-3, Madv. § 115 f.

This philological uncertainty is not removed by the practical usage of the forms in question. In the present passage it is quite an open question (cf. 127 note), but *faxo* is often used where a fut. simple would naturally stand, and in 847-8 it is a direct coordinate of *faciam*, fut. The subjunctive form is never used as a perf., but always as a fut. subj.; cf. the common phrase *di faxint* expressive of a wish, Hor. Sat. 2. 3. 38 *cave faxis*, and the use of *ausim*. Cf. 854 note. Vergil, Livy,

80   ADELPHI.

Ovid, and Horace occasionally employ these forms, and *di faxint* is found even in Cicero. As regards construction *faxo* is followed four times in Terence by the fut. ind.; cf. Phor. 308 *iam faxo hic aderit*, ib. 1055, Eun. 285, 663, thrice by the pres. subj. here and infra 847 placed after the subj., and Andr. 854. It is also constructed with an acc. and a perf. part. pass., e.g. Haut. 341 *ademptum tibi iam faxo omnem metum*. There is no certain instance of the fut. ind. after *faxo* in Plautus, and the Augustan writers always use the subjunctive construction.

Translate, 'I will soon make him anxious to take the money.'

211-12. Notice the assonance and alliteration; cf. 57 note.

Translate, '... that you have had some little fighting-match with my master. SA. I never saw a fight worse matched.'

nescio quid. Cf. 79 note.

214. **tua culpa.** Ablative: cf. Hec. 228.

morem gestum oportuit, sc. *morem a te gestum esse oportuit*, 'you ought to have humoured.' Cf. 218, 431, 672, 706, Andr. 641, etc. The acc. and inf. is the regular construction after *oportet* in Terence, e.g. Haut. 536 *haec facta ab illo oportebat*, *esse* being omitted with a perf. inf. pass. Cf. Andr. 239.

215. **qui potui**, 'how could I have...' Cf. 179 note.

usque os praebui, sc. *verberibus*, 'even submitted my person to downright violence.'

216. **in loco**, 'at the right time.' Cf. 827, 994.

218. **esses morigeratus**, a rare word once used by Cicero. In the MSS. *atque* is read after *paululum* 217. Some editors print 218 *Atque adulescenti morigerasses*, introducing the active form once found, Pl. Amph. 981. But *atque* is almost certainly the addition of a copyist who noticed the asyndeton.

219. **ne ... faeneraret**, 'that it (*istuc*) should not pay you with interest:' cf. Phor. 493 *faeneratum istuc beneficium pulchre tibi dices*. Augustan writers prefer *faeneror* to *faenero*.

220. **rem**, 'your fortune.' Cf. 95.

abi, 'go to:' an expletive, sometimes used in a good sense, more often threatening or contemptuous. Cf. 564, 620, 703, 765. Cf. *age* 271.

222. **mallem potius.** Note the emphatic doubling of the comparative, as in Andr. 427 *omnes sibi malle melius esse quam alteri*.

223. The sense is, 'come, come, I know you well enough: as if twenty minae were either here or there to you, provided you oblige so good a customer as Aeschinus.'

usquam, 'either here or there:' cf. *nullo loco habere*.

224. **praeterea autem**, a pleonastic phrase, such as is very common in Terence. Cf. 246, 255, 259, 268, 294, 306, 366, 525, 541, 785.

aiunt proficisci. Cf. 203 note. In English we similarly use a present tense to express an immediately future action.

225. hoc, taken by some editors as abl. of cause, dependent on *pendet*. It seems more natural to consider it as acc. after *scio*.

226. spero is parenthetical: cf. 79 note, 411.

tamen. Cf. 110.

hoc ages, 'you will do this bit of business,' i.e. the sale of the music-girl to Aeschinus.

227. nusquam pedem, sc. *feram*.

228. inieci scrupulum homini, lit. 'a small pointed stone,' hence 'anxiety,' 'doubt,' 'uneasiness.' Cf. Andr. 940, Phor. 1019. A neuter form *scrupulum*, or *scripulum*, is used as the smallest division of weight, $\frac{1}{24}$ of an ounce.

229. ut in ipso articulo oppressit, sc. *me*, 'how he has caught me at the very nick of time.' For the indic. cf. 195 note.

232. agam, sc. this dispute with Aeschinus.

233. refrixerit. The metaphor is taken from iron cooling. Cf. the English proverb, 'strike while the iron is hot.'

234. quor passu 's? 'why did you let the matter rest?'

perdere, 'to put up with the loss.'

235. persequi, sc. *causam*.

236. id quod ad te rediturum putes, 'your expected gains,' i.e. from your venture to Cyprus.

237. hocine incipere Aeschinum? Cf. 38 note.

241. face, archaic for *fac*, used by Plautus and Terence at the end of lines. Plautus sometimes also writes *duce, dice*, for *duc, dic*, but not *fere* for *fer*. Terence always employs the syncopated forms except *face* as mentioned above, and -*duce* in composition in 482 *abduce*, 910 and 917 *traduce*. After the time of Terence the shortened forms are always found.

242. conradet. Cf. Phor. 40 *ei credo munus hoc conraditur*.

243. sorte, 'the principal.'

246. etiam insuper. Cf. 224 note.

defrudat, so A altered by a later hand to *defraudat*, other MSS. *defrudet*. Compare *occludo*, etc. from *claudo*, and *frustra*.

247. numquid vis? A common formula of leave-taking. 'Is there anything you want me for?' Cf. Phor. 151, Pl. Trin. 192. Hor. Sat. 1. 9. 6.

251. Ctesiphonem. Terence always so declines Greek names in -ῶν, -ῶντος: cf. Phor. 463 *Antiphonem*, ib. 899 *Demiphonem*, etc.

253. quid quod te oro? 'what about my request?' Syrus takes Sannio's money, but is careful to avoid making any definite promise in return.

G

ACT II. SCENE 3.

Ctesipho has heard that the music-girl with whom he is in love has been rescued from Sannio by Aeschinus. He is brimming over with gratitude to his brother, and comes to find him.

254. abs was a collateral form of *ab* (cf. ἐκ, ἐξ), used before words beginning with *c, q, t*. As early, however, as Plautus *abs* is rarely found except before *te*. Cicero always wrote *abs te* up to about B.C. 55. Occasional uses of *abs* in later authors, e. g., Livy, are probably intentional archaisms. In *as-pello, as-porto, as-pernor* (for *as-spernor*), the *b* has fallen out. Cf. Pl. Pers. 159 *abs chorago*.

    quivis=*quovis*. Cf. 179.

    beneficium. For the scansion cf. 72 note.

255. vero enimvero. Cf. 168, 224 notes. *Enĭmvero* is the regular scansion in Terence, though Phor. 528 seems to be an exception.

    id demum, 'that especially.' Compare the emphatic use of *adeo*.

258. praeter alios, 'more than other people.' This use of *praeter* is not found in Augustan writers.

259. The meaning is, 'that no human being has a brother more eminently endowed with the highest qualities.'

    homini nemini, a colloquial pleonasm. Cf. Phor. 591, etc.

    For **artes** = 'qualities' cf. Andr. 33.

    primarum artium principem. Perhaps no phrase exactly parallel can be adduced; though Liv. 8. 21 *principes sententiarum consulares* is similar.

260. ellum = *ecce illum*. The fuller forms *eccillum, eccillam, eccillud* are used by Plautus, e. g. Trin. 622. *Ecce* is also compounded with cases of *is* and *iste*, e. g. *eccum* (common), *eccam, eccos, eccas, ecca, eccistam*. Sometimes *eccum* is followed by another accusative. Cf. 389, 553, 720, 890, 923.

    hem is here an exclamation of joy, more commonly of surprise, grief, alarm, anger, etc.

    Spengel scans *Aeschinŭs | ubĭst ĕllum*, on the ground that the last syllable of the fourth foot of an iambic tetrameter is regarded as at the end of a verse. It is to be observed, however, that Terence frequently does not end a word with the fourth foot, e. g. in three of the six preceding lines. So that it is doubtful whether Spengel's scansion is more likely than *Aeschinŭs ubist ĕllum*, since it involves the very unusual lengthening of *-us* before a vowel. See Introduction on Metres. Cf. Andr. 957.

261. quid sit? Cf. 84 note.

    festivom caput! 'delightful fellow!' Cf. Andr. 371 *ridiculum caput*, infra 983, 986. It is a translation of Gr. κάρα, similarly used.

262. The text gives what was probably the original reading of **A** (except that *putavit* is printed for *putarit*), but the line has been materially altered by a later hand. Most other MSS. read *qui omnia sibi post putarit*. Most editors adopt *quin omnia*, etc., the only reading known to Donatus, explaining *quin* as *quine*. But in all the passages quoted by them where *-ne* is affixed to the relative, e. g. Andr. 768, Phor. 923, Pl. Rud. 272, ib. 538, there is a question; here there is not. It seems therefore most simple to take *quin* as a corroborative particle, 'indeed;' in which case the asyndeton between this and the following clause is emphatic and natural.

Note the following uses of *quin*:

(1) 'Why not?' either in direct or indirect questions.

(2) With imperatives. This use was a natural development of the first; for *quin taces*? is equivalent in sense to a command: e. g. 533, 543.

(3) In the common sense, 'but that,' after verbs expressing doubt, prevention, and the like, with a negative: e. g. 257, 294.

(4) As a corroborative particle, 'indeed,' 'verily:' e. g. here and 734: sometimes further strengthened by *etiam*.

263. **meum amorem**, the reading of all MSS., has been altered to *laborem* by many editors on account of the metre. I have preferred Bentley's emendation of *sese* for *se*.

264. **nil potest supra**, sc. *esse* vel *dici*.

foris, not elsewhere in Terence in the singular.

crepuit. Greek doors opened outwards, and so it was customary before leaving a house to knock against the door as a warning to persons in the street. The door was said *crepare*, *concrepare*, Gr. ψοφεῖν. A person knocking from within or without was said *pellere fores*, Gr. κόπτειν, κρούειν, cf. 638, 788; or, if violent, *pulsare*, *pultare*, Gr. δράσσειν, cf. 633, 637.

ACT II. SCENE 4.

Aeschinus comes out to see how affairs are progressing. Ctesipho is very anxious to hush the matter up, and Sannio is now willing to come to terms, and has to be content with a promise of the cost-price.

265. **me quaerit.** Sannio, with comical readiness, appropriates to himself the epithet *sacrilegus*.

266. **quid fit?** 'how goes it?' a common form of salutation, like *quid agitur*. Cf. 373, 883, 901.

267. **in tuto**, etc. Cf. Andr. 845 *omnis res est iam in vado*.

omitte vero, '*do* lay aside.'

tristitiem = *tristitiam*. Both here and 358 *nequitiem* **A** alone has preserved the archaic form, though in both places a recent corrector has written *a* above the E. There is no certain instance of *tristities* elsewhere. Cf. *mollities, mundities, luxuries, segnities, durities* (Speng.).

268. **hercle vero.** Cf. 224. *hercle* commonly used by men, *ecastor* by women.

qui habeam, 'since I have;' for *qui* causal cf. 368.

269. **germane,** 'my own brother.' Cf. 957.

in os. Cf. Fr. *au nez,* Gr. κατὰ στόμα.

270. **adsentandi,** sub. *causa*: cf. Liv. 9. 45 *pacis petendae*. This construction is probably due to a literal translation from the Greek of the inf. with τοῦ, e.g. τοῦ κολακεύειν. The writers of the silver age often employ it.

quo habeam gratum, 'because I am really grateful;' lit. 'from the fact that I hold it (your service) worthy of thanks.' For *quo* cf. 825. The subj. represents the idea as a mental conception.

271. **age,** 'come, come,' often used thus as a simple expletive, e.g. 553, 626, 941. Cf. *abi* 220.

norīmus = *noverimus*. The ancient long quantity is found elsewhere in Plautus and Terence, e.g. Phor. 772, also in Ovid.

272. The text gives the reading of all the MSS. The phrase *res rediit* is so common, e.g. Phor. 153, 359, 686, etc., that many editors have suppressed one *paene* and introduced *rem*, altering *scisse* to *rescisse*. But *redire* = 'to be reduced to' is used with a personal subject, e.g. Caes. B. G. 3. 93, ib. 5. 48; and there seems scarcely sufficient ground for so considerable an alteration of the MSS., especially as the sentence is a mere continuation of *nos paene sero scisse*.

hoc mihi dolet. *Dolere* is also used by the comic writers impersonally, e.g. Phor. 162. Cf. 451, 682, 733.

273. **nil,** acc. of respect dependent on *auxiliarier*.

auxiliarier. Cf. 200 note.

274. **pudebat,** 'I was ashamed,' sc. to speak of it.

275. **paene e patria,** sc. *fugere*. Ctesipho had intended to follow the music-girl to Cyprus.

quaeso, an older form of *quaero*, as *asa* for *ara*.

276. **tandem,** 'pray;' often thus used to emphasise a question, e.g. 665, 685.

nobis, ethic dative.

277. **ad forum,** i.e. where the bankers carried on business.

278. **insta,** 'press the matter on.' Syrus, as before, is very anxious not to commit himself.

ne tam quidem! with a gesture, δεικτικῶs. Cf. 163. 'Not even so much,' i.e. not at all. It must be confessed that this gives an unusual meaning to *tam*, but it seems easier than (with Dziatzko) to read *non tam quidem, quam vis ; etiam maneo otiosus hic*.

279. **ne time.** This archaic construction is not common in Terence, and disappeared altogether in later Latin, except rarely in the poets. Cf. 802.

280. **at ut omne reddat**, sc. *timeo*.

282. **absolvitote**, plural because Aeschinus is included. The fut. imperative is very rarely used, as here, of a single act.

siet. Cf. 83 note.

283. **aliqua**, sc. *via*.

permanet, 'should leak out.'

285. **lectulos**, 'couches' for an entertainment.

287. **ita, quaeso**, 'yes, please.' In conversational language *ita* often = 'yes,' e.g. 521, 570, 642, 655. Cf. 543 note.

hilarem. Terence uses elsewhere *hilarus -a -um*, which was the usual form in old Latin: cf. 756, 842. All MSS. here give *hilarem*.

sumamus = *consumamus*, 'let us spend.'

ACT III. SCENE I.

Aeschinus, who had secretly married Sostrata's daughter Pamphila, had not paid lately his usual visits. Sostrata expresses to Canthara, the old family nurse, her great anxiety.

289. **edepol**, 'by Pollux,' shorter form *pol* 293. The prefix is formed from the interjection *e*, found in *ecastor*, and perhaps a syncopated vocative of *deus*.

modo, 'just now,' applied to present time, is rare and ante-Augustan. Cf. 87.

mea tu, sc. Pamphila, an endearing expression.

primulum, the diminutive implies the very first beginning. Cf. 898.

291. **Geta**, a confidential slave.

293. **numquam unum.** Cf. 332.

294. **semper**, pleonastic after *numquam*. Cf. 224.

295. **e re nata**, 'under the circumstances.'

296. **quod ad illum attinet**, 'as far as regards him.' This limiting sense of the relative is very common, and may be followed either by an indic. or subj. according to the shade of meaning implied. Cf. 423, 427, 511, 519, 641, 692, 963, Roby, §§ 710–711.

297. **genere**, the reading of all MSS., has been altered by Bentley, followed by many editors, to *ingenio*, on account of *familia*. But *genere* refers simply to noble birth, *tanta familia* to the wealth and social importance of the family. See 89, where *familia* is used in its original sense of 'household,' meaning the slaves, not wife and children.

298. **siet.** Cf. 282 note.

Act III. Scene 2.

Geta, having seen the violent abduction of the music-girl, concludes that Aeschinus has fallen in love with some one else and will desert Pamphila. He rushes on, greatly excited and longing to vent his righteous indignation on the head of Aeschinus. His agitation is such that only with difficulty can Sostrata elicit an account of what has happened.

299. **quod**, lit. 'with reference to which;' cf. 162 note. *Quod* appears in A B C E F P, *cum* altered to *quod* in D, *quod cum* in G. Many editors, on the analogy of Pl. Capt. 516, Rud. 664, substitute *quom* for *quod*. But as *quod* gives a good sense, there seems hardly sufficient justification for this plausible emendation. Translate, 'matters are now at such a pass, that if . . .' Such a sentence as this shows us *quod* in a transition state between a pronoun and a conjunction.

300. **auxili**. This form of the genitive from nouns in *-ius*, *-ium*, was general until the latter part of the Augustan age. Vergil only uses the form in *-ii* once, A. 3. 702 *fluvii*, Horace never. Ovid was the first to introduce the longer form, for metrical reasons. However adjectives in *-ius* do not contract the genitive.

301. **filiae erili** = *filiae erae*. Cf. Andr. 602 *erilis filius*.

302. **circumvallant**, sc. *nos*.

emergi. This verb is sometimes used transitively, more often intransitively, and so impersonally in the passive, as here. Cf. Andr. 562 *spero . . . facile ex illis sese emersurum malis*, Eun. 555. The mixture of metaphors in *circumvallant* and *emergi* is perhaps intentional in the mouth of a Thracian slave.

potest, impersonal, as commonly in Terence. Cf. 350 note.

304. **hocine saeclum!** acc. of exclamation; cf. 758. The particle *-ne* stands here, as with the acc. and inf., in indignant exclamations. Cf. 37 note.

305. **quod**. Cf. 162 note.

sic, δεικτικῶς, as often in the comic poets.

306. **illum**, pleonastic after *quem*, for the sake of emphasis. Cf. Verg. A. 1. 1-3, 5. 457

Nunc dextra ingeminans ictus nunc ille sinistra.

310. **vix sum compos animi**, 'I am scarcely master of myself;' not identical with *compos mentis*, which means 'sane.'

312. **evomam**. Cf. 510.

313. The MSS. give '*satis . . . dum illos ulciscar modo*,' which does not scan. The insertion of *meo* seems the best emendation.

NOTES. LINES 299–330.

satis supplici, 'vengeance enough.' Cf. 300 note.

314. seni. Micio rather than Demea is probably meant, as he had brought up Aeschinus.

illud scelus, i.e. Aeschinus.

316. The text gives the reading of **A**, except that the copyist carelessly wrote INTERRASTUEREM; all other MSS. have *Sublimem medium arriperem et capite primum in terram statuerem*, which some editors alter to *capite pronum* . . .

capite in terram statuerem, 'I would set him down again head foremost.' Cf. Lucret. 4. 473 *qui capite ipse suo in statuit vestigia sese,* 'who stands upon his head.'

medium, 'by the waist.' Cf. Andr. 133 *median mulierem complectitur*.

317. dispergat, not *dispergeret*, because the clause is explanatory of the kind of action described by Geta, without referring to any particular time. Cf. 782.

318. praecipitem, sc. *eum*. Note the tendency to analytic forms, cf. 241.

319. ruerem, transitive, 'I would hurl down.' Cf. Haut. 369, Verg. G. 1. 105, etc., infra 550.

320. impertiri. The deponent form is preserved by **A**: not used by any Augustan writer.

321. It seems to have been a common practical joke at Athens to delay slaves who were going on messages by calling out to them on false pretences.

quaerito. Cf. 81 note.

322. Notice the fourfold alliteration and assonance. Cf. 1 and 57 notes.

oppido opportune, 'in the very nick of time.'

323. trepidas . . . festinas. Cf. 305 *timidum et properantem*.

quid festinas . . . recipe. Most modern editors, on the authority of the grammarian Asper, give these words to Canthara against the MSS. There is, however, nothing strange in Sostrata's address *mi Geta* to an old and confidential slave, especially under such alarming circumstances.

324. animam recipe, 'take breath.'

ergo. Cf. 172 note, 326.

326. quid is ergo, sc. *fecit*?

328. id occulte fert, 'carries it on secretly;' opposed to *prae se fert*.

ipsus, archaic for *ipse*, common in Terence.

329. satine = *satisne*, B *satin*, G *satisne*. Cf. 336 *sanun*.

330. nostrumne Aeschinum? 'What? our Aeschinus!' An

elliptical phrase ; understand *hoc fecisse*. The character of the sentence, at once interjectional and interrogative, is well shown here. Cf. 38 note.

331. **nostram vitam omnium.** So all MSS.; we should have expected *nostrum* gen. pl.

332. **unum numquam.** Cf. 293. Some editors suppress *erant* and scan this line and the next as trochaic septenarii.

333. **patris**, i. e. the adopted father Micio. By receiving the infant in his arms Micio would sanction the marriage.

335. **ac potius . . . prospice,** 'and rather consider what course should be adopted in the future.'

quod ad hanc rem opus est. The constructions of *opus* and *usus* are,

(1) *Personal*, with the thing needed in the nom. as a subject. The phrase may be completed by *ad* with an acc., as here and Andr. 740, or by an ablative which is sometimes a perf. part. pass. as in 996 *quid facto opus est*, more rarely a supine as in 740. Roby, § 507, suggests that this may be a combination of *quid est opus* and *quo facto est opus*. Cf. 429, 625.

(2) *Impersonal*, with the thing needed in the abl., which may be a noun, adjective, or participle, very rarely in the gen. (twice in Livy) or acc. (twice in Plautus). In place of an abl. an infinitive, or acc. and infinitive, is sometimes found ; e. g. 625, and the person needing is always in the dat. Cf. 342, 601.

Notice the alliteration.

339. **proferimus.** Note the present instead of the future, as often in Terence, rarely in Augustan writers. Cf. Zumpt § 510.

infitias ibit, 'he will deny it,' viz. his relations with Pamphila. In later Latin this phrase is seldom used without a negative.

sat scio, parenthetical. Cf. 79 note.

340. **si maxume fateatur,** 'if he should confess it ever so much.'

342. **tacito est opus.** Cf. 335 note.

minume gentium, 'not for the world!' *gentium* is a partitive genitive after *minume*. Cf. *nusquam gentium*, ποῦ γῆς ; etc. 540.

343. **Sostrata.** Terence usually preserves the long termination of Greek names in -*a*, except of dissyllables, as Getă.

agis, the reading of **A** ; cf. 195 note : other MSS. *agas*.

344. **potis est,** 'is possible.' *Potis* may refer to a subject of any gender, or may be used impersonally. The neut. *pote* is similarly employed, but usually without *est*, while with *potis* the *est* is nearly always expressed. *Potis* rarely refers to a plural subject, and neither *potis* nor *pote* is found in classical prose. Cf. 521, 625.

347. **anulus.** A ring was similarly relied on as a means of identification in Hec. 572-4, 829.

349. **intercessisse**, 'has passed between us.'

350. **experiar**, 'I will go to law.'

quid istic? Cf. 133 note.

cĕdo ut melius dicas: a phrase of doubtful meaning:

(1) 'I give in, granting that your suggestion is better' (*ut* concessive).

(2) 'I allow that your suggestion is better,' i.e. *cedo = concedo* (Bentley).

Some editors read *dicis* with Priscian, translating

(3) 'I give in since your suggestion is better.'

All MSS. give *accedo ut melius dicas*, against the metre: *cedo* is Bentley's correction.

potest. The impersonal use of *potest* in this and similar phrases is so general, that we have admitted it here, as in Andr. 861, on the authority of Donatus. Cf. 302 note, 700, 743, 909.

351. **eius**, sc. Pamphilae. *Cognatus* may be followed by a gen. or a dat. The gen. is here natural, as *cognato* is already in the dat. Menander makes Hegio the brother of Sostrata.

352. **Simulo**, sc. Sostrata's deceased husband.

summus, 'nearest friend.'

ACT III. SCENE 3.

Demea has heard that Ctesipho was a party to the abduction of the music-girl. In his anger and distress he meets Syrus, who adroitly draws out the old man's foibles and parodies his moral maxims.

355. **disperii**, a strengthened form of *perii*. Cf. Phor. 1011 *distaedet*, Pl. Trin. 932 *discupio*, infra 610 *discrucior*.

Ctesiphonem. Cf. 252 note.

356. On the apparent discrepancy see note at beginning of Act II. Sc. 1.

357. **potest** may be impersonal, or Aeschinus may be understood as the subject.

358. **qui aliquoi rei est**, 'who is worth something,' dat. of the complement.

eum repeats *illum*, as in 741. Cf. 306, 315. Some editors place the comma after *etiam*, translating 'who is as yet worth something.'

360. **eccum.** Cf. 260 note.

ire video in later Latin would be *euntem video*. Cf. Andr. 580 *video exire*.

hinc, 'from him.' Cf. 413 *unde*.

scibo. Terence uses *scibo* for 1st pers., *scies* for 2nd pers. (except in Haut. 996 and perhaps Eun. 805), *scibit* for the 3rd pers. Cf. 780.

362. **atque,** 'and yet.' Cf. 40 note.

grege, 'gang.'

363. **quaeritare.** Cf. 81 note.

364. **omnem rem,** sc. the abduction of the music-girl.

seni, sc. Micio.

Syrus of course intends Demea to overhear his soliloquy.

365. **haberet,** used absolutely, as ἔχειν with adverbs. The nom. is of course *res*. The ordinary *res se habet* is found Phor. 820, etc.

enarramus. There is no good reason for considering this as a contracted form of *enarravimus*. It is quite regular to have an imperf. subj. dependent on a historic present.

366. **nil quicquam vidi laetius,** 'I never in my life saw anyone better pleased.' The emphatic pleonasm '*nil quicquam*' has many parallels in Terence, e. g. 38, 528, 716, Andr. 90, Phor. 80, etc.

367. **hominis,** sc. Micio.

368. **qui id dedissem.** Cf. 268.

369. **disrumpor,** 'I burst with rage.' Cf. 355.

adnumeravit, 'paid down' to Sannio.

370. **dedit in sumptum,** 'he gave us to spend.'

minae. The Attic mina = 100 drachmae, i.e. about £4 of our money.

371. **ex sententia,** 'to my liking.' Cf. 420.

373. **quid agitur.** Cf. 266 note.

374. **quid agatur.** Cf. 84 note.

375. **rationem,** 'conduct.'

ne dicam dolo, 'to speak the honest truth.'

376. In A *atque* is found before *absurda*, in defiance of the metre. It is doubtless a gloss inserted by some one who did not see how much more forcible the asyndeton here is.

Dromo and Stephanio (380) are slaves employed in the kitchen. Possibly Terence intended Syrus to be accompanied by them on his return from the forum with the provisions (286), as Sosia appears at the beginning of the Andria. In that case the conger and the other fish would have been seen by the audience carried across the stage.

381 **macerentur,** 'soaked.'

di vostram fidem, sc. *imploro*. Cf. 746 note.

382. **utrum studione ... an.** 'In early Latin, and even in Cicero, *-ne* may be used in addition to *utrum* in the first member of a disjunctive question, to mark more clearly the opposition of the two

clauses. *Ne* is separated from *utrum* by one or more words. Horace Epod. 1. 7 first uses *utrumne*.

utrum ... habet, 'which is it?' 'does he (Micio) do it on purpose, or does he think it will be creditable to him?'

385. militatum. The usual resource for a young Athenian, driven by debt or despair to leave his country, was to take service under the flag of one of the numerous Asiatic princes, between some of whom war was almost sure to be going on. Cf. Pl. Trin. 598–9 *Ibit statim aliquo in maxumam malam crucem Latrocinatum, aut in Asiam aut in Ciliciam.* Haut. 117.

388. penes vos, 'in your house:' cf. Pl. Trin. 733.

389. ellam. Cf. 260 note.

habiturus, sc. Aeschinus.

390. dementia, a nominative, 'Such is his infatuation:' cf. Eun. 525 *ut est audacia*.

haecine fieri. Cf. 38 note.

393. pernimium. Notice the intensive force of *per*. Cf. 566, 567, 702, Andr. 265 *peropus*.

394. quantus quantu's, 'from top to toe.'

395. somnium, 'a mere nothing.' Cf. 204.

396. aut is sometimes used in adding the consequence of denying a former proposition: 'or else,' 'otherwise.' Cf. Roby § 872.

397. olfecissem, 'I should have got wind of it.'

coeperet, the archaic imperf. subj. attested by Priscian. The MSS. reading *coeperit* is contrary to syntax. This utterance seems hardly consistent with 355–360. It may be another result of the 'contamination.'

398. siet, sc. Ctesipho.

399. quisque, meaning Demea and Micio. *Uterque* would have been more exact.

400. quid eum? sc. *narras*. 'What about him?' Cf. 777. *Narro* in Terence may mean 'I tell of.' Cf. 777, Andr. 466, etc.

401. hunc, sc. Demea.

402. Oh, qui egomet produxi. 'Oh, 'twas I myself who took him out.' Cf. προύπεμψα.

403. iratum, acc. after *produxi*.

404. quid autem. Cf. 185 note.

405. istac, 'that which you speak of.'

406. numerabatur. Cf. 369.

408. haecine, etc. Cf. 38 note.

411. spero. Cf. 226.

similis maiorum suom. Cf. 96 note.

suom = *suorum*, as deûm, divôm; cf. Gr. gen. in -ων. Cf. 793.

413. unde, 'from whom:' cf. 361 *hinc*.
  fit sedulo, 'I spare no pains.'
418. istaec res est, 'that's the way.'
421. cautio est = *cavendum est*. In Plautus these verbal substantives retain the government of the original verb, e.g. Poen. 5. 5. 29 *quid tibi hanc digito tactio est;* in Terence they are usually followed by a genitive or a separate clause, as here; cf. Andr. 400, Phor. 293: but the dat. is found in Andr. 44 *exprobratio est inmemori benefici*. Notice throughout the whole of this speech the admirable parody of Demea's recent words, a parody which on the stage would extend to his tones and gestures.

422. tam flagitium est quam..., 'is a crime as heinous as...' Cf. 379.

423. quod queo, 'as far as I can.' Cf. 296 note.

425. hoc lautum est parum, 'this is not washed clean enough.' The use of *lautus* in its literal sense is rare. See, however, Pl. Pseud. 162–3 *facite ut offendam parata, Vorsa, sparsa, tersa, strata, lauta, structaque omnia ut sint*. Notice that even the sound of Demea's '*hoc laudi est*' is parodied.

427. pro mea sapientia. A play on the double sense of *sapere*, 'to taste,' and 'to know' is here intended. 'According to the dictates of my taste.'

429. quid facto usus sit, 'what ought to be done.' Cf. 335 note.

431. 'But what are you to do? As a man is, so you must humour him.'

432. numquid vis? Cf. 247 note.

433. recta, sc. *via.* Cf. 574.
  nam, etc. The connexion is, 'you do right to go; for...'

435. abeo. The present tense is often used in colloquial Latin, as in English, to express the immediate future. Cf. 538, 549, 757.
  quam ob rem = *cuius ob rem*, by attraction.

437. frater = *Micio*: **istoc** = *Aeschinus*.
  viderit. The future perfect is thus used to put off or abandon the question in point. Here, as in Andr. 892 *viceris*, it implies indignant concession. Cf. Verg. A. 10. 743 *Nunc morere; ast de me divom pater atque hominum rex Viderit*. In such cases it is a virtual imperative. Cf. Roby § 667. Translate, 'let my brother himself see to the fellow, since so he wishes it.'

439. tribulis noster, 'of our tribe,' Gr. ὁμόφυλος or δημότης.
  si satis cerno, 'unless my eyes deceive me.'
  vah! is here expressive of admiration, as in Andr. 589.

441. ne (less correctly *nae*), an affirmative particle always joined to pronouns or their adverbs, sometimes with the addition of *hercle, edepol*, Gr. νή, ναί. Cf. 540, 565.

442. **antiqua virtute**, 'of old-fashioned worth,' abl. qualifying *civium*. Cf. Andr. 817 *pol Crito antiquom obtines*. Roman conservatism shows itself in *antiquos* = 'good old.'

443. 'The state would be slow to reap any harm from him.'

quid is very rarely thus put for *aliquid*, not depending on *si, ne, num*, etc.

Act III. Scene 4.

Demea overhears the conversation of Hegio and Geta, at first supposing it referred to the affairs of the music-girl. He is, however, soon enlightened, and is strongly urged by Hegio to do full justice to Pamphila of his own free will. Demea, however, gives no decided answer, but goes off to vent his wrath on Micio.

448. **quid narras?** '*mirantis est non interrogantis*' (Don.) 'Is it possible?'

familia. Cf. 297 note.

449. **inliberale,** 'ungentlemanly:' cf. 57, 664. For the construction see 38 note.

450. 'This conduct is certainly not like your father.'

pol is more commonly used by women than by men.

paternum. Cf. 74 note.

dedisti. For this sense, 'to do,' 'to inflict,' cf. Andr. 143 *quid facias illi, qui dederit damnum an malum?*

451. **dolet.** Cf. 272 note.

452. **pater,** sc. Micio, his adoptive father.

eius is scanned as a monosyllable.

453. **hic,** an adverb.

454. **illos,** sc. *facere*; cf. 505.

haud sic auferent, sc. *hanc rem*, 'they shall not carry off the matter thus,' i.e. with impunity. Cf. Andr. 610 *sed inultum numquam id auferet*.

457. **ille senex,** sc. Simulus. Cf. 352.

458. **cave dixeris,** 'don't mention the word;' i.e. *deseris*. Gr. εὐφήμει: lit. take care lest you may have said what you ought not.

459. **satis pie,** 'in common honour;' 'consistently with my duty towards the family.'

462. **quid autem?** Cf. 185 note.

463. **boni,** 'a man of right feeling.'

464. **liberalis.** Cf. 57 note.

functus officium est: *fungor* governs the acc. in Plautus and

ADELPHI.

Terence, with one exception, infra 603, where the MSS. give the abl. Conversely *fruor* is constructed with the abl. in Terence, except in Haut. 401, where the acc. is found. For *potior* cf. 871, for *utor* 815.

465. noras = *noveras*.

466. aequalem, 'of our own standing.' Cf. ὁμήλικα.

quid ni? 'of course.' Cf. 573, 662.

468. an. Cf. 136 note.

quicquam. So all MSS. and Donatus: though *quam* in A has been added by a later hand. But *an* is followed by *quisquam* in six other passages of Terence, e. g. Phor. 279, 1009, and by *quis* never.

471. humanum est, 'it is human nature.'

472. ipsus. Cf. 328.

ultro, 'of his own accord:' lit. beyond what might have been expected of him; contrasted with *sponte*, which merely means 'willingly.' Cf. 595, 596.

476. ille bonŭs, a proceleusmatic. See Introduction on Metres. *Bonus* is often used ironically, e. g. 556, 722.

nobis, an ethic dative: 'our good gentleman.'

si dis placet, 'heaven save the mark!'

477. quicum = *quacum*. Cf. 179 note.

479. in medio est, 'is at hand.' Cf. Phor. 16. Gr. ἐν μέσῳ κεῖται.

480. ut captus est servorum, 'as slaves go:' *captus*, 'capacity.'

482. abduce. Cf. 241 note.

quaere rem, 'extort the truth.' The evidence of slaves, both at Athens and at Rome, was taken under torture.

484. non negabit, sc. Aeschinus.

coram ipsum cedo, 'put him face to face with me:' *coram* adverb. No writer before Cicero used *coram* as a preposition.

489. illae, sc. Pamphila.

490. vos vis, sc. *legum*. So A with C D. The other MSS. read *vos ius*. At first sight *ius* seems more natural. But (1) the greater authority of A: (2) the alliteration *vos vis voluntate*: (3) Phor. 214 *vi coactum te esse invitum, lege, iudicio*: also Liv. 26. 12. 8 *qui indignitate vim ac ius magistratui quem gerebat dempsisset*, lead me to retain *vis*.

491. ut vobis decet. This was the regular construction of *decet* in archaic Latin, which reappeared in the silver age. In Terence three constructions are found after *decet*:

(1) The dative, as here and 928.

(2) The acc. and inf., infra 506, 948, 954-5.

(3) The acc. alone, as in Augustan Latin, probably by ellipse of an inf., e. g. Andr. 421 *facis ut te decet* (sc. *facere*), ib. 445.

493. **summa vi,** 'with all my might,' as in 490 *vis* here refers to legal proceedings, not, as is usual, to physical force.

  illum. Cf. 457 note.

 495. **educti.** Cf. 48 note. All MSS. read *educati*.

 497. **experiar.** Cf. 350.

 499. After this line the MSS. of the Calliopian recension insert from Phor. 461 *Is quod mihi de hac re dederit consilium, id sequar.*

 500. **hoc ... cogites,** 'see that you keep this in mind.' Cf. 808.

 501. **quam ... agitis,** 'in proportion as you fare most easily.' *Quam* with the superlative in place of *quo* with the comparative is rare. It is found once elsewhere in Terence, and may be a literal translation of ὅσῳ ... τοσούτῳ followed by superlatives. Many editors supply *vitam* after *agitis*, but the familiar phrase *quid agis?* 'how do you do?' is quite sufficient to account for the above use. Cf. Haut. 997 *quam maxime huic vana haec suspicio erit, tam facillume,* etc.

 503. **aequo animo aequa noscere,** 'fairly to recognise what is just and fair.'

 506. **decet te facere.** Cf. 491 note.

 507. **me indicente,** 'without warning from me.' The particle *in* prefixed to verbs seems to have a negative sense only with participles, as above and Phor. 951 *quod dictum indictum est,* Andr. 782 *ioculariuin in malum insciens paene incidi,* ib. 603, etc.

  utinam hic sit modo defunctum, 'I only pray that this may prove the end.'

  hic, adverb.

  defunctum sit, here an impersonal passive. Cf. Phor. 1021 *cupio misera in hac re iam defungier.*

 510. **evomam.** Cf. 312.

Act III. Scene 5.

Hegio speaks a few reassuring words to Sostrata, before going in search of Micio.

 511. **istam,** sc. Pamphila.

  quod potes, 'as far as you can;' acc. of limitation. Cf. 423 note.

 514. **si est is facturus.** All MSS. read *si est facturus*, which requires a most irregular hiatus between *si est.* Translate, 'if it prove that he is prepared to do his duty.' For a similar periphrasis cf. Phor. 270, Hec. 501.

ADELPHI.

ACT IV. SCENE I.

Syrus had sent off Demea, as he supposed, safely into the country, but Ctesipho is alarmed at the possible consequences of the trick. Syrus is suggesting a way out of the difficulty, when Demea appears in person, having accidentally heard that Ctesipho is not at his country house.

517. **dic**, 'tell me about it.'
    sodes = *si audes*, 'if you please.' Cf. 643, 766.
518. **nunc quom maxime**, 'now at this very moment.' Cf. Andr. 823, Phor. 204. In all these cases, however, *quom maxime* might be taken as qualifying the verb which follows.
    utinam quidem, sc. *ita sit.*
519. **quod**, 'as far as.' Cf. 423 note.
    velim as a potential subjunctive, 'I would wish,' is followed indifferently by a pres. or perf. subj. or by an infinitive.
520. **triduo hoc perpetuo**, 'within three whole days from this.'
521. **istoc**, abl. after *rectius*.
    potis. Cf. 344. Syrus means, 'may he never get up again.'
    ita, 'just so.' Cf. 287 note.
522. **misere**, 'distractedly,' similarly used as an intensive adverb in 667, 698. Terence often thus links together two adverbs.
523. **male**, also used intensively, e.g. Hec. 337.
525. **revorti iterum**, a pleonasm.
527. A reads EGOKODIETOTO, etc. Many editors, considering that the object of *vidi* must be expressed, have altered *hodie* to *hoc te*, or accepted the reading of the later MSS. *quem ego hodie*. The ellipse of *te*, however, has a parallel in that of *eum* in 525 and in 608, the context in both cases making the sense certain: while to pass from indirect to direct speech, when the clauses are connected by a relative, would be scarcely possible.
528. **in mente est.** Here A has *in mentem*, all other MSS. *in mente*, while in the parallel passage Haut. 986 A with D G read *in mente*, the other MSS. *in mentem*. The MS. authority being so evenly balanced the reading most in harmony with ordinary syntax has been chosen.
    numquam quicquam. Cf. 98 note.
    tanto nequior, sc. *es*, 'the more fool you.'
529. **quid postea?** 'what then?' Cf. 649, 929. The simple-minded and honourable Ctesipho does not at first catch the drift of the slave's suggestion.
530. **hisce ... sit**, 'so that you may have had business with them.'
531. Note the weakness of Ctesipho's character. He is a mere tool in the hands of Syrus.

533. quin. Cf. 262 note.

sensum, 'disposition.'

534. fervit. In early and late Latin *fervo, fervĕre* was the common form. Vergil retains *fervĕre* in three passages.

535. laudarier. Cf. 200 note.

537. em tibi autem, 'look out for yourself:' *tibi* is an ethic dative. Cf. 790, Andr. 842 *em Davom tibi*. For *autem* cf. 185 note.

lupus in fabula. An allusion to some fable in which a wolf appears just as he is being spoken of. Plautus Stich. 577 and Cicero ad Att. 13. 33. 4 quote the same proverb. 'Talk of the devil.'

538. agimus. Cf. 435 note.

videro. Cf. 127 note. 'I will see to it.'

539. nusquam tu me, sc. *vidisti*.

potin = *potisne es*. Cf. 344, 521.

ACT IV. SCENE 2.

Syrus further dupes Demea, and by false information sends him off to the other end of the city to find Micio.

540. ne. Cf. 441.

nusquam gentium. Cf. 342.

541. praeterea autem, pleonastic.

a villa mercenarium, 'one of the farm-servants.' *a* signifies 'proceeding from,' and so 'belonging to.' Cf. 585 *lectulos in sole*.

543. verum, 'yes.' An affirmative answer may also be expressed by *ita, etiam, sane, factum, vero, scilicet*, etc.; or by repeating the verb, e.g. *hoc facies? faciam*; or by a pronoun, e. g. *hoc facies? ego vero*. Cf. 287 note, 561, 729, 752.

quin. Cf. 262 note.

544. malum, interjectional, 'the plague on it.' Cf. 557.

quid infelicitatis hoc, sc. *est?* 'What ill-luck this is!'

nequeo satis decernere, 'I can't quite make it out.'

547. obnuntio, the regular word for announcing bad news or an evil omen. Cf. Cic. Phil. 2. 33. 83 *augur auguri, consul consuli obnuntiasti*.

549. redeo... viso. For the tense cf. 435 note. *Viso*, 'I am going to see.' Cf. 889 *proviso*, Andr. 404 *reviso*.

550. inruat, 'should force his way in.' This is the only instance of *inruo* as a transitive verb, though *ruo* is so used several times. Cf. 319 note, Eun. 599 *proruont se*.

etiam taces? '*do* be quiet.' Gr. οὐ μὴ σιωπήσει;

551. numquam hodie. For this emphatic phrase cf. 570. Verg. E. 3. 49: ib. A. 2. 670.

552. me in cellam aliquam concludam, 'I will shut myself up into some room.'

553. age, 'all right.' Cf. 271.

eccum. Cf. 260 note.

554. hic, 'in this place,' i. e. 'in this family.'

si sic fit, 'at this rate.'

556. quid ais, a common phrase in Terence, used:

(1) As a request for information, when a remark has not been heard, or in asking for a person's opinion. Cf. 920.

(2) As an exclamation of surprise or anger at some remark which seems scarcely credible. Cf. 570.

(3) To introduce a new point in conversation, or to call attention, like *dis donc*. Cf. the present passage, 'I say, my good sir.'

559. usque occidit, 'has half killed me.' Cf. 90.

em. Cf. 169.

discĭdit, from *discindo*, not *discīdit* from the very rare *discido*, as some editors suppose on insufficient metrical grounds.

561. produxe = *produxisse*. A similar syncopation (*is* being omitted) of verbs whose perf. indic. end in *-si* or *-xi*, is used by Latin poets:

(1) In the second pers. sing. perf. indic. (often), e. g. 599, 604, 689, 940, 952; and second pers. plur. (rarely).

(2) In perf. infin. Cf. Haut. 32 *decesse*, ib. 1001 *iusse*, and *nosse* often, e. g. 648.

(3) In all persons sing. and first pers. plur. of pluperf. subj.; but none of this last set occur in Terence.

The syncopation of *-avisti*, *-avissem*, etc., into *-asti*, *-assem* is too common to require detailed notice.

aibas = *aiebas*. Terence seems to have used *-ibam* or *-iebam* for the imperfect of the fourth conjugation indifferently: e. g. Andr. 38 *servibas*, Phor. 83 *serviebat*; but always *scibam, nescibam*. The shorter form was sometimes employed by later poets, e. g. *lenibat, nutribant, vestibat* by Vergil; *audibat, mollibat* by Ovid. *Aibam,* etc., probably represents the colloquial pronunciation in the time of Terence.

factum. Cf. 543 note.

562. non puduisse. Cf. 38 note.

563. modo, 'quite lately.'

puerum tantillum, 'a little fellow so small,' with a gesture.

564. laudo, 'bravo.'

patrissas, 'you are your father's own son,' or 'you are a chip of the old block.' Greek authors use πατριάζω; the form πατρίζω, cf.

NOTES. LINES 551–583.   99

μηδίζω, etc., is mentioned by Priscian. This word is twice found in Plautus. Cf. Pl. Men. 11-12 *graecissat, atticissat, sicelissat.*

abi. Cf. 220 note.

565. **ne.** Cf. 441 note.

566. **perquam!** 'Oh very!' Cf. 393, 567.

servolum, 'a poor slave.' Note the force of the diminutive termination. Cf. 27 note, 647.

568. **te esse huic rei caput,** 'that you are at the bottom of this affair.' Cf. Andr. 458.

570. **hodie numquam.** Cf. 551.

quid ais? Cf. 556 note.

ita. Cf. 543 note.

572. **dic ergo.** Cf. 172 note.

573. **hac deorsum,** 'down this way.' *Hac,* sc. *via,* is Bentley's correction for *hanc* in the MSS. Cf. 574, 575, 577, 580, 582.

deorsum, dissyllabic in Terence and Lucretius.

quidni noverim? Cf. 466 note.

574. 'Pass this way straight up the street.' Cf. Shakes. Mer. of Venice 2. 2.

platea, 'a street.' Gr. ἡ πλατεῖα ὁδός. In spite of the derivation the scansion is *platĕa*: Hor. Ep. 2. 2. 71 *purae sunt plateae.* So κρηπῖδα crĕpĭdam, πρόλογος prōlogus.

sursum ... ubi. Note the hiatus rendered possible by the full stop. To avoid this some editors read *sursus.* Cf. *deorsus deorsum, prorsus prorsum, rursus rursum, vorsus vorsum, advorsus advorsum* (676).

575. **clivos deorsum vorsum est,** 'there is a slope right down in front of you.'

576. **ibi angiportum propter est,** 'there hard by is an alley.' *Angiportus,* mas. of the fourth decl. and *angiportum,* neut. of the second decl. are both found. The word was applied to those passages leading off the streets through a sort of doorway, common in most old towns. Sometimes such a passage is a thoroughfare, sometimes a 'cul de sac.'

577. **illi.** Cf. 116 note.

579. **censen hominem me esse?** 'what an ass I am!' *Homo* here means a person with the ordinary intelligence of a human being, as opposed to *pecus.* Cf. 107 note.

580. **erratio,** 'chance of going wrong.'

581. **huius,** scanned as one syllable.

582. **hac recta platea.** Cf. 574.

ad Dianae, sc. *templum,* a common ellipse.

583. **portam,** showing that Demea was to go to the very extremity of the city.

lacum. Near the gates of a city were usually pools of water, both for the use of cattle, and also in case of any hostile attempt to fire the gates.

584. **pistrilla**, diminutive of *pistrina*, 'a small flour-mill.'

585. **lectulos in sole**, 'some out-of-door seats,' for the *solarium* or place for basking in the sun. Cf. 541.

faciundos dedit, 'he has ordered.'

587. **silicernium**, 'old dry-bones;' lit. 'a funeral feast,' so, as a term of abuse, one who can be of no service except to be the occasion of a funeral feast.

588. **Aeschinus odiose cessat**, 'the delay of Aeschinus is most annoying.'

589. **in amore est totus**, 'is over head and ears in love.' Cf. Hor. Sat. 1. 9. 2 *nescio quid meditans nugarum ; totus in illis.*

590. **adibo**, sc. the dinner-table.

unumquicquid, rarely found for *unumquidque* : cf. Pl. Trin. 881.

bellissumum, 'nicest :' *bellaria* was the word used for dessert, including fruit, sweet-meats, wine, etc., and this word is doubtless intended to be suggested by *bellissumum*.

591. **carpam**, 'I will pick out.'

cyathos. The *cyathus* was a sort of ladle used for transferring wine from the large bowl (*crater*) in which it was mixed to the drinking-cups (*pocula* or *calices*).

paulatim hunc producam diem, 'I will leisurely lengthen out the day.'

Act IV. Scene 3.

Hegio has found Micio and told him the whole story. Micio at once promises ample redress. This draws from Hegio warm commendation, which Micio modestly declines.

593. **meum officium**. This may be scanned by considering *meum* as a monosyllable by synizesis, and then eliding it, for which there are many parallels, or by shortening *officium*, and scanning the first foot as a proceleusmatic. See Introduction.

594. **nisi si**, as in *quasi si*, εἰ μή εἰ, πλὴν ἐάν, the hypothetical force of the first word is forgotten. Caesar, Livy, and Cicero occasionally use *nisi si*. Cf. Andr. 249, Pl. Trin. 474.

595. **sibi ... ultro**, 'that they are wantonly insulted.' Cf. 472 note.

si ... expostules, sc. *eam iniuriam*, 'if you complain of;' cf. Andr. 639.

597. **te aliter**, sc. *esse*. 'I have never thought you to be other than you are.'

599. **dixti**. Cf. 561 note.   **mulieri**, i. e. Sostrata.

600. There is no need to suppose a verse dropped out after this line, as some editors do.

601. **opus est facto.** Cf. 335 note.

bene facis. On account of the repetition of these words in 604 this line is supposed by some to be interpolated or corrupted. But it may have been a mere oversight.

602. **illi,** sc. Pamphila.

603. **tuo officio fueris functus.** Cf. 464 note. The change of tense from *relevabis* to *fueris functus* has led Fleckeisen to read *relevaris*; but a similar change is found elsewhere, e. g. 980–1, Andr. 570.

604. **dixti.** Cf. 561 note. Note the hiatus accounted for by the punctuation.

607. **inpotentiam,** 'poverty,' ἅπαξ λεγόμενον in this sense. Cf. Xen. Oec. 20. 22, ἀδυναμία.

claudier. Cf. 200 note. This is the reading of A, for which Bentley conjectured *ludier*. But 'hindered' or 'baulked of their rights' gives a fair sense, and is supported by Andr. 573, Eun. 164. The Calliopian MSS. give *neglegi*, which is an evident substitution for the more difficult *claudier*.

608. **te ipsum,** sc. Micio, the object of *purgare* being understood to be the recent conduct of Aeschinus.

ipsi, sc. Sostrata; cf. 598.

coram. Cf. 484 note.

placabilius est, 'is the better way to appease them.' Verbal adjectives in *-bilis* often have an active force in archaic Latin, e. g. Phor. 961 *id nosmet indicare placabilius est*, rarely in the Augustan period, e.g. Verg. G. 1. 93 *penetrabile frigus*.

ACT IV. SCENE 4.

Aeschinus has accidentally heard that Sostrata and Pamphila believe him to be false. He is deeply distressed, yet cannot tell them the whole truth without betraying his brother's secret. At length he plucks up his courage and knocks at Sostrata's door.

For the Metres of this short *Canticum* see Introduction and table of Metres. The irregularity of the lines is intended to express the disturbed and conflicting feelings of the young man, and the predominance of iambic metres from 610–615 is suitable to his despondent mood.

610. **discrucior animi.** Cf. 355 note.

animi is a locative, like *humi, domi*, etc.: cf. Phor. 187, infra 655.

hocine obici. Cf. 38 note.

611. **quid me faciam?** 'what I shall do with myself?' *Facere, fieri,*

and *esse* are thus constructed with the abl. without a preposition, sometimes also with the dat. or rarely with *de* and the abl. Cf. Andr. 614 *quid me faciam?* ib. 709 *quid me fiet?* Phor. 137 *quid te futurum est?* Andr. 143 *quid facias illi, qui dederit damnum aut malum?* infra 996.

siet. Cf. 83 note.

615. **turba,** 'confusion,' 'entanglement,' 'coil,' often in this sense in Terence.

617. **anus,** sc. Canthara: *anus* is usually an elderly woman of the lower orders, *matrona* an elderly lady.

id ... indicium fecit = *id indicavit.* Cf. 939.

619. **iam partus adsiet.** The interrogative particle is here omitted in an indirect question, as elsewhere in a direct question, e.g. 136.

620. **eone,** 'whether for that reason.'

abi, 'avaunt.' Cf. 220 note. Some editors punctuate *abi, abi: iam, Aeschine, satis ...*

623. **me reprehendi,** 'I restrained myself.'

624. **fieret palam,** sc. the matter. Such a change of the subject is common in conversational language.

625. **quod minume est opus.** Cf. 335 note.

626. **efferri,** 'should get abroad.'

ac mitto, 'well, I put that aside.' Five of the Calliopian MSS. read *age* for *ac*.

potis est. Cf. 344 note.

ut ne = *ut non.* A negative result is similarly expressed by *ut ne* Andr. 699, Pl. Trin. 105, etc. Terence also uses *ut ne* = *ne* to express negative purpose, e.g. Andr. 259: so Cicero in Verr. 2. 4. 28 *nam rex celatum voluerat ... ut ne multi illud ante perciperent oculis quam populus Romanus.*

627. Aeschinus fears that Sostrata and Pamphila may not believe the story that he carried off the music-girl for his brother's sake.

ipsum id is acc. after *credant.*

629. **adeo.** Note the uses of *adeo:*

1. 'So far.'
    (*a*) Of space, Phor. 55 *res adeo redit.*
    (*b*) Of time, Andr. 660–2 *numquam destitit ... Suadere, orare, usque adeo donec perpulit.*
    (*c*) Of circumstance, Andr. 245 *adeon hominem esse invenustum aut infelicem quemquam, ut ego sum.*
2. As an intensive particle with
    (*a*) pronouns, as here and 797 (common);
    (*b*) adjectives or adverbs, 989 *nunc adeo* (νῦν γε);
    (*c*) conjunctions, especially *ut,* infra 987;
    (*d*) verbs, Andr. 759 *propera adeo puerum tollere.*

3. 'Moreover,' 'besides,' (rare).

The intensive use of *adeo* is not uncommon in Vergil, e. g. E. 4. 11 *teque adeo*, G. 1. 94 *multum adeo*, A. 3. 203 *tres adeo . . . soles*, 'three whole days.'

    non me . . . Cf. 38 note.

630. ut ut erat gesta. Cf. 195 note.

631. cessatum usque adhuc est, 'it has been put off and off all this time.'

    nunc porro, 'now from this moment.'

633. perii! 'ah me!'

    pultare. Cf. 264 note.

634. aperite aliquis, 'open, some one of you, . . .'

Act IV. Scene 5.

638. pepulisti. Cf. 264 note.

641. istas, sc. *pepuli*.

    quod sciam. Cf. 423 note.

642. ita, 'just so.' Cf. 287 note.

643. Micio has been thus playing a part to discover if his adopted son has still the honourable instincts of a gentleman. Aeschinus feels how badly he has treated Micio in concealing all his love-affair from him, and blushes with shame. This is one of the most delicate touches in the play. Cf. Menan. ἐρυθριῶν πᾶς χρηστὸς εἶναί μοι δοκεῖ.

    salva res est, 'it is all right.'

    sodes. Cf. 517 note.

646. advocatum. The legal term 'advocate' is here used because the supposed proceeding was one enjoined by law; cf. 652, Pl. Trin. 1161.

647. pauperculae. For the force of the deminutive termination see 566 note.

648. ut opinor eas non nosse te. This construction is a mixture of *ut opinor, eas non nosti*, and *opinor eas non nosse te*. Cf. Phor. 480-1 *ut aibat De eius consilio sese velle facere nosse*. Cf. 561 note.

649. quid tum postea? Cf. 529.

652. huic leges cogunt nubere hanc. Cf. Phor. 125-6 *lex est ut orbae qui sunt genere proxumi Eis nubant, et illos ducere eadem haec lex iubet.* Such girls were called ἐπίκληροι: cf. case of Ruth.

654. Mileti, a celebrated Ionian colony in Caria. A man might be an Athenian citizen, and so subject to Athenian law, though residing for the time in a colony.

655. ita. Cf. 287.

    animo male est, 'I am distracted.' *Animo* is an abl.; cf. the locative *animi*, e. g. 610.

656. **quid illas censes**, sc. *dicere*.

nil enim. Cf. 168 note.

660. **nonne** is rarely used by Terence, who prefers *non* or *-ne*. Cf. 83, 94 notes.

post ea, i. e. after the events just mentioned by Micio. For *post ea* Bothe conjectured *poscere*, reading *videtur* with **A**. It would be a great improvement, but the MSS. are unanimous for *post ea*.

661. **an.** Cf. 136 note.

662. **quid illam ni**, by tmesis for *quidni illam*. Cf. 466 note.

664. **inliberaliter.** Cf. 57, 449 notes.

665-6. **tandem.** Cf. 276 note.

animi depends on *quid*. 'What, pray, do you think will be the feelings of that wretched man?'

qui illa consuevit, so **A**, the other MSS. *qui cum illa consuevit*, against the metre. *Illa* is governed by the preposition in *consuevit*, but it must be admitted that the construction is very harsh and unusual.

667. **misere.** Cf. 522.

668. **praesentem**, so Servius (ad Aen. 4. 83), the MSS. *praesenti*, which seems impossible.

670. **qua ratione istuc?** 'how so?'

671. **auctor his rebus quis est?** 'who gave his consent to this?'

At a formal wedding the parents, guardians, and near relatives were present as *auctores*; cf. Cic. pro Clu. 5. 14 *nubit genero socrus, nullis auspicibus, nullis auctoribus*.

672. **alienam**, 'another man's bride.' Pamphila, as an orphan, belonged by law to her next of kin. Cf. 652 note.

aliena may, however, merely mean 'an entire stranger.'

an sedere oportuit. Cf. 214 note. *Sedere*, 'sit idle.'

673. **tam grandem**, 'of such an age.' Cf. 930, Andr. 814 *grandiuscula*.

dum depends on *expectantem*.

hinc illinc, 'from heaven knows where.' '*Proverbialiter hinc illinc*,' Don.: the MSS. *huc illinc*.

676. **advorsumne.** Terence writes *-ne* where a later writer would put *num*.

677-8. **quid ista nostra**, sc. *sunt*? 'what is this affair to us?'

679. Notice the change of metre as Micio drops the part which he has been playing, and speaks in his true character with real feeling.

681-3. 'May I deserve your love, while your life lasts, my father, no less sincerely than I am grieved to have been guilty of this fault, and am ashamed to see you!'

me tui pudet. The gen. after *pudet* is more often the fault of which one is ashamed, e.g. 391-2, but cf. Pl. Trin. 912 *deum me hercle atque hominum pudet*.

684. **liberale.** Cf. 57, 449 notes.   **sies.** Cf. 83.

685. **tandem.** Cf. 276 note.

687. The second *magnum* is not found in the MSS., but it is necessary to the metre, and its omission would be a very natural error by a copyist.

688. **cedo,** 'tell me.' Cf. 123.

689. **circumspexti ... prospexti.** Cf. 561 note. 'Did you show any caution, or take any precaution?'

691. **qua resciscerem** depends, like *quid fieret? qua fieret?*, on *prospexti*, and should be translated before the clause *si te ... proloqui*.

692. **quod quidem in te fuit,** 'as far indeed as in you lay.' Cf. 423 note.

695. 'I should hope that you will not be equally thoughtless of the rest of your affairs.'

socors is also found with the gen. in Tac. H. 3. 31.

696. **duces uxorem hanc.** No marriage was recognised as formally complete until the assent of the legal guardian was obtained.

697. **nunc ludis tu me?** so A. This requires a hiatus between *me* and *ego*; to avoid which most editors follow the later MSS., *num ludis tu nunc me* or *num ludis nunc tu me*. But see Introduction xxix.

698. **misere.** Cf. 522 note.

700. **quantum potest.** Cf. 350 note.

702. **perbenigne,** sc. *dicis*, 'you are very kind.' Cf. 393 note.

quid? used like *quid ais* (cf. 556 note), to arrest attention and introduce a new point.

703. **periit, abiit, navem ascendit,** so A; five Calliopian MSS. read *abiit, periit*, etc. But the order in A is not illogical. Micio's hypothetical Milesian being no longer wanted is summarily suppressed, the words *abiit, navem ascendit*, being playfully added to give the farce a suitable ending. Translate, 'he is done with—gone, embarked.'

abi. Cf. 220 note. Some editors translate *abi* literally as in 699.

705. **quo.** The corresponding *eo* must be supplied before *magis*.

706. **quae opus sunt.** Cf. 335 note.

ut dixi, sc. in 699.

708. **morem gereret.** Cf. 214 note.

709. **hem** is here expressive of admiration and affection.

711. **sciens cavebo,** 'forewarned, forearmed.'

712. **siem.** Cf. 83 note.

ACT IV. SCENE 6.

Demea returns from his wild-goose chase, furious at the trick which Syrus has played upon him.

713. ut is sometimes used by the comic writers, like *utinam*, to introduce imprecations; e. g. Eun. 302.

715. perreptavi, a word suited to the pace of an old man. 'I have trudged all over the town from end to end.'

717. aibat. Cf. 561 note. The MSS. read *aiebat*.

domi, i. e. at Micio's house.

718. obsidere usque, 'to sit on and on.'

ACT IV. SCENE 7.

Demea fiercely assails his brother about the newly-discovered relations of Pamphila and Aeschinus. Micio treats the matter with the utmost coolness. The young couple are to have quarters in his house, where even the music-girl is to be accommodated. Demea is reduced to helpless silence, in despair at his brother's infatuation.

720. eccum ipsum. Cf. 260 note.

722-3. boni, ironical, as in 476, 556.

DE. Nova, Capitalia, so the MSS. Several editors follow Bothe's conjecture, *MI. Ecce autem nova. DE. Capitalia.* But there is no reason to alter the MS. reading.

nova, 'unheard of.'

723. ohe iam! sc. *desine*. 'Oh, that's enough:' a form of impatient or ironical remonstrance: cf. 769.

727. non. Cf. 94 note.

non insanis? We have a similar usage in colloquial language, 'to be mad' = to be beside oneself with anger.

malim quidem. All existing MSS. give these words to Micio. Donatus, however, mentions that some attribute them to Demea, and this arrangement would yield an excellent sense: sc. *malim quidem te insanire*.

729. scilicet. Cf. 543 note, 751.

730. enim. Cf. 168 note.

fert, 'suggests,' 'requires.' Cf. 53, 839, Andr. 832 *incepi dum res tetulit: nunc non fert.*

731. illinc huc, i. e. from her house to mine.

732. istocine. The strengthening affix *-ce*, joined with the interrogative particle *-ne,* is thus written; cf. 758. It is especially used by Terence in indignant questions or exclamations.

oportet, sc. *fieri*.

quid faciam amplius? Micio comically pretends that Demea blaming him for not doing enough, instead of too much.

733. dolet. Cf. 272 note.

734. hominis = 'human,' in 736 'humane.' Cf. 107 note.

735. **fiunt nuptiae**, 'their wedding is being arranged.' The secret and informal marriage of Aeschinus and Pamphila was to be ratified by a public and legal ceremonial.

737. For omission of the interrogative particle see 136 note.

738. **quom non queo.** This is a good instance of the way in which the temporal sense of *quom* passes into the causal. Cf. 139 note.

739. **quasi quom**, very rarely found thus together.

ludas tesseris. The same comparison is used by Alexis, a poet of the Middle Comedy, who died at Athens about 285 B.C.,

τοιοῦτο τὸ ζῆν ἐστὶν ὥσπερ οἱ κύβοι.

Plato Rep. 10. 604 C anticipates Terence in his application of the figure, ὥσπερ ἐν πτώσει κύβων πρὸς τὰ πεπτωκότα τίθεσθαι τὰ ἑαυτοῦ πράγματα, ὅπῃ ὁ λόγος αἱρεῖ βέλτιστ' ἂν ἔχειν. Three dice, numbered like our own, were thrown from a *fritillus*. *Tali* (ἀστράγαλοι), were knuckle-bones, originally played as with us, but afterwards numbered on four sides and thrown like dice, but five at a time. The best thrown with *tesserae* was three sixes, (cf. Aesch. Ag. 33), with *tali* when all turned up different (*iactus Veneris*).

740. **opus est iactu.** Cf. 335 note.

741. **arte ut corrigas.** Cf. Hor. Sat. 2. 8. 84 *Nasidiene, redis mutatae frontis, ut arte Emendaturus fortunam*. Corrigas, 'manipulate,' *corrector*, 'fine manipulator!'

743. **quantum potest.** Cf. 350 note.

744. **gratiis**, in later Latin *gratis*.

745. **neque est**, sc. *abicienda*.

746. **pro divom fidem**, sc. *imploro*. The interjection *pro* does not affect the case of the word before which it stands. Cf. 111.

749. **ita me di ament**, 'so help me heaven.'

ut, 'when.'

750. **facturum credo**, *te* omitted. Cf. 77 note.

quicum = *quacum*. Cf. 179 note.

cantites. This passage seems to allude to Roman customs and feeling rather than Greek. At Athens music and dancing were a regular part of education, and were commonly practised in every-day life. At Rome such frivolities were left to slaves, to be performed for the amusement of their masters. So strong was the Roman prejudice against dancing, except in certain religious ceremonies, that Cicero (pro Mur. 6) writes, *nemo fere saltat sōbrius, nisi forte insanit*. Demea's sneers, therefore, would have fallen rather flat upon a Greek audience, but such conduct in the head of a Roman house would have been considered an indecent outrage of propriety; and when even this taunt fails to touch Micio's sense of shame, we can well understand Demea, in his utter despair and disgust, really thinking his brother to be out of his right mind. Cf. 761 *senex delirans*. On the above supposition, we have here perhaps the nearest approach to a Roman allusion in any of Terence's plays. See Introduction xvi.

751. **scilicet.** Cf. 729 note.

752. **restim ductans.** A rope-dance is mentioned by Livy 27. 35. § 14 *in foro pompa constitit : per manus reste data virgines sonum vocis pulsu pedum modulantes incesserunt.* Demea represents Micio as leader of such a dance.

753. **probe.** A form of assent. Cf. 287.

754. **non.** Cf. 94 note.

pudent. Cf. 84 note.

757. **hos,** masculine, because Hegio is included.

convenio ... redeo. Cf. 435 note.

761. **Salus,** daughter of Aesculapius. Abstraction and personification were the special characteristics of Roman religion. In other words, the Romans personified qualities, natural phenomena, etc., and then worshipped them as gods. See Mommsen, vol. i. c. xii.

ACT IV. SCENE 8. [ACT V. SCENE 1.]

Demea's anger and disgust are still further increased by the insolence of Syrus, who comes out of the house more than half drunk.

It is quite impossible to believe that Terence intended the action of the play to be interrupted at line 762 by the termination of the Act, while on the other hand there is a well-defined break after the Scene marked in the MSS. as V. 3. The origin of the mistake was probably as follows: From the beginning of Act IV. (line 517) to the end of the play there are 481 lines. The natural division after line 854 gives 338 lines to Act IV. and only 143 to Act V. To a copyist, who would be much more concerned with the number of the lines than the thread of the plot, this might well appear bad management, which could be improved by making the Acts as nearly equal as possible. This is exactly what has been done, 246 lines having been assigned to Act IV. and 235 to Act V. Assuming therefore the original commencement of Act V. to have been at line 855, the Acts and Scenes have been numbered accordingly, though, for convenience of reference, the old notation has been preserved in brackets.

763. **edepol.** Cf. 289 note.

Syrisce, an endearing diminutive.

764. **munus administrasti tuom,** 'you have done your duty.' We have a similar colloquial use of the phrase with reference to eating and drinking.

765. **abi.** Cf. 220. It is here expressive of satisfaction.

766. **prodeambulare**, ἅπαξ λεγόμενον. Wagner conjectures *prodambulare*, on the analogy of *prodesse, prodire*.

lubuit. Augustan writers nearly always use *libitum* or *lubitum est* as the perf. of this word, and all the Calliopian MSS. here give *libitum est*.

sis = *si vis*. Cf. 517 note.

768. **quid fit?** 'how goes it?'

769. **ohe iam.** Cf. 723.

verba fundis? 'are you wasting words?' Cf. 433-4.

sapientia (cf. 394), 'wiseacre.'

770. **dis** = *dives*. The contracted form is very rare in the nom. sing., but common in other cases.

771. **tuam rem constabilisses**, 'you would have put your fortune on a firm footing.'

exemplo is Bentley's suggestion for the corrupt reading of A, *exempla*; other MSS. have *exemplum*.

775. **nollem exitum**, sc. *esse a me*. Cf. 165 note. Of course *exitum* is here used impersonally.

Act IV. Scene 9. [Act V. Scene 2.]

A slave sent by Ctesipho comes to summon Syrus. Demea catches the name, and, in spite of Syrus' opposition, rushes into the house.

777. **quid Ctesiphonem hic narrat?** 'What does he say of Ctesipho?' Cf. 400 note.

779. **parasitaster**, ἅπαξ λεγόμενον, a diminutive of contempt.

paululus is similarly used by Livy to express smallness of stature. Cf. 35. 11. § 7 *equi hominesque paululi et graciles*. Translate, 'a miserable little scrap of a hanger-on.'

780. **nostin? iam scibo.** 'Do you know him? I will soon find it all out.' Cf. 360 note.

781. **non.** Cf. 94 note.

mastigia, 'you scoundrel;' a common term of abuse in Plautus, not used elsewhere by Terence. Gr. μαστιγίας. Cf. *verbero*.

782. **cerebrum dispergam.** Cf. 317.

783. **comissatorem**, acc. of exclamation.

785. **dum.** Cf. 196 note.

interea is pleonastic after *dum*.

786. **villi**, ἅπαξ λεγόμενον, contracted from *vinulum*, a diminutive of *vinum*. It is a partitive gen. after *hoc*, 'this little drop of wine.' Cf. 870

ADELPHI.

Act IV. Scene 10. [Act V. Scene 3.]

Micio encounters Demea half frantic at the discovery that it is Ctesipho who is in love with the music-girl. Micio with great difficulty calms him down, and extracts an ungracious consent to be present at the marriage ceremonies of Aeschinus and Pamphila.

788. **ubi vis**, temporal, 'whenever you wish.'
  quisnam. Cf. 168 note.
  a me, 'at my house.' Cf. Andr. 226 *sed Mysis ab ea egreditur*.
  pepulit, rarely used of a person coming out. Cf. 264 note.

789. **quid faciam? quid agam?** These expressions are not quite synonymous: *quid faciam?* 'what act am I to do?' *quid agam?* 'what measures am I to adopt?' The former refers to the physical act; the latter includes the mental conception.

790. **em tibi**. Cf. 537.

791. **ilicet**, 'the game is up,' i.e. the secret about Ctesipho is out. *ilicet = ire licet* was the formula of dismissal from an assembly, funeral, or other ceremonial gathering; see Conington's note on Verg. A. 6. 231. Thence, 'let us be gone,' 'all is over.' Cf. Phor. 208 *ilicet: quid hic conterimus operam frustra?* Eun. 55 *actum est, ilicet, peristi*. The later MSS., except D, which has *licet*, read *scilicet*, which most editors connect with *id nunc clamat*.

792. **paratae lites**, 'we are in for a row.' Cf. Phor. 133 *mihi paratae lites*. Ctesipho would naturally be the principal object of Demea's rage, though Micio and Aeschinus would come in for their share.
  succurrendum est, 'I must to the rescue.'

793. **nostrum liberum**, gen. plur. Cf. 411.

796. **rem ipsam putemus**, 'let us look into the case on its merits.'' *Putare* = 'to reckon accounts,' thence 'to investigate,' 'to think over.'

797. **ex te adeo est ortum**, 'it was from you yourself that the proposal came.' Cf. 629 note. For the proposal in question see 129–132.

799. **recipis**, 'harbour.' Cf. Cic. Mil. 19. 50 *praedarum receptor*.

800. **numqui**. Cf. 179 note.

801. The order is *numqui minus aequom est idem ius mihi (tecum) esse quod mecum est tibi?* 'Is it in any way less just ...'

802. **ne cura**. Cf. 279 note.

803. **verbum**, 'proverb.' Cf. Andr. 426 *verum illud verbum est, volgo quod dici solet*.

804. **communia ... omnia**, Gr. κοινὰ τὰ τῶν φίλων, said to be a Pythagorean maxim. It is quoted in Latin by Cicero de Off. 1. 16. 51; in Greek by Martial 2. 43. 1 and 16.

806. **ausculta paucis**, sc. *verbis*. The analogy of Andr. 29 *paucis te volo*, Pl. Trin. 963 *te tribus verbis volo*, etc., makes it more probable that *paucis* is here an ablative than a dative. The same phrase occurs Andr. 536.

807. **sumptum**, attracted into the case of the relative. This 'inverse attraction' is not uncommon in Terence when the antecedent is placed in the relative clause, e.g. Andr. 3, ib. 26.

808. **hoc** is object of *cogites*.

809. **pro re tollebas tua**, 'you were bringing up according to your means.' At Rome it was the custom to lay a new-born infant at the feet of its father, who raised it in his arms if he wished to acknowledge it. Hence *tollere* = (a) to acknowledge as one's child, (b) to bring up as one's child. Cf. Andr. 219 *quidquid peperisset, decreverunt tollere*.

812. **obtine**, 'keep to.' Note that *obtinere* = *adipisci*, 'to obtain,' is not found before Cicero, and is not at all common in any writer.

antiquam. Cf. 442 note.

813. **conserva, quaere, parce**, 'hoard, scrape, and save.'

814. **gloriam tu istam obtine**: so A and D (first hand). If the reading be correct the awkward repetition of *obtine*, 812 and 814, as of *bene facis* 601 and 604, are almost the only instances of careless writing in this most polished of Terence's plays.

815. **mea ... utantur.** Terence elsewhere constructs *utor* with an ablative, but *abutor* with an accusative. Cf. 464 note. Here the acc. might be due to 'inverse attraction.'

evenere, 'has come in to them.'

816. **de summa nil decedet**, 'there will be no diminution of your capital.' A reads *decedit*.

hinc, i.e. from my fortune.

817. **de lucro**, 'as clear gain.' The preposition *de* often signifies the whole from which a part is taken.

819. **dempseris.** Cf. 127 note.

820. **mitto rem**, 'I do not mind about the money.'

consuetudinem, 'morals,' with special reference to the company they keep.

ipsorum. A alone has *amborum*. The contrast with *rem* makes *ipsorum* so much more forcible that the text has followed the later MSS. and Donatus.

821. **istuc ibam**, 'I was coming to that point.'

822-3. The order is *ex quibus, (duo quom idem faciunt), coniectura facile fit saepe ut possis dicere*.

825. **quo.** Cf. 270.

827. **eos**, omitted in A, is inserted on the authority of the other MSS. because (1) the ellipse would be awkward, (2) the copyist of A was

rather prone to admit small words, e. g. 826 *in*, (3) the same combination of letters occurring in VIDEOSAPERE his eye might very easily be deceived.

in loco. Cf. 216 note.

828. scire est, so all MSS. except A by error SCIREET. It is a Graecism, natural enough to one translating ἔστι γνῶναι or some such phrase. Translate, 'one can see.' *Est* = 'it is possible' is not uncommon in the Augustan poets, e. g. Horace Sat. 1. 5. 87 *quod versu dicere non est*, Verg. G. 4. 447 *neque est te fallere quicquam*. Many editors, following Lachmann, alter *scire est* here to *scires, seiris* (for *siveris*) or *sciris*, and Haut. 192 *credere est* to *crederes*.

liberum. Cf. 57 note.

830. redducas. There is little doubt that this was the correct spelling in early Latin. Lucretius lengthens the first syllable, and the double *d* often appears in MSS., e. g. here in D, Hec. 605 in A.

ab re, 'in money matters:' *ab* denotes here, as often, the direction from which the matter in question is viewed. Cf. *a fronte, a tergo*, etc.

at enim. Cf. 168 note.

835–6. quod, 'wherein,' an acc. of respect. Cf. 162 note.

ne ... modo, 'only take care lest ...'

nimium strengthens *bonae*, 'those exceedingly fine arguments of yours.'

tuae istae. The addition of *istae* emphasises *tuae*, and gives moreover a contemptuous turn to the sentence.

837. tuos iste animus aequos, 'that unruffled disposition of yours.'

838. istaec, 'those fears.'

839. exporge = *exporrige*, 'smooth the wrinkles,' 'unruffle.'

fert, 730 note.

841. cum primo luci. In old Latin *luce, luci*, and *lucu* are all found as ablatives or locatives of *lux*, which before the classical period was either masculine or feminine.

de nocte, 'by night:' *de* indicating the time from which the action dates. Cf. 965 *de die*.

843. pugnaveris, a colloquial expression explained by Donatus as *magnam rem feceris*. 'You'll have won the day.' Cf. Pl. Epid. 3. 4. 57 *homo es, pugnavisti*. The fut. perf. accurately expresses the result which follows the fut. simple *abstraham*.

844. illi = *illic*. Cf. 116 note.

845. videro. Cf. 127 note.

846–7. The order is *Atque ibi faxo (ut) sit coquendo et molendo plena favillae, fumi ac pollinis.*

faxo. Cf. 209 note.

852. **sies**, a causal subjunctive. Cf. 83 note.
853. **ego sentio**, 'I have some feelings.'
854. Notice that *I* is elided, and that *rei* in both cases is made monosyllabic by synizesis and then suffers elision. See Introduction on Metres xxviii, xxix.

ACT V. SCENE I [4].

Demea reflects on the practical results of his own and his brother's manner of life. He sees that it is pleasanter to be affable and liberal than morose and parsimonious, and resolves to turn over a new leaf. But if he has erred in being too stern, so has Micio in being too complaisant. Therefore Demea undertakes a practical demonstration of his brother's failings by an extravagant travesty of his easy-going principles.

855. The assumption by Demea of a lighter character is reflected in the metre by the change from iambics to trochaics.

numquam . . ., etc. 'No one has ever had a rule of life so well thought out.'

subducta, lit. 'calculated.' *Subducere rationem* = to cast up an account by subtracting the debit from the credit total. Cf. Pl. Capt. 192 *subducam ratiunculam*: often in Cicero.

ita qualifies the whole sentence, not merely *bene*, as then *tam* would have been used.

857. **ut . . . nescias**, 'so that you find yourself ignorant of.' This clause expresses the general result of the teachings of experience as set forth in 855-7, and does not depend immediately on *moneat*, which, in the sense of 'warning that you do not know,' would of course be followed by an infinitive, not by *ut* with a subjunctive.

scisse, so A, the other MSS. *scire*: but the perf. gives a good sense, 'which you may imagine that you have understood.'

860. **prope iam excurso spatio**, 'when now my course is almost run.' This metaphor from the race-course as applied to life is found in many authors, ancient and modern.

861. **facilitate**, 'affability.'

864. **nulli laedere os**, 'to affront no-one to his face,' 'to tread on no one's corns.' The infinitives here are historic, as in the parallel passage Andr. 62 seqq. Cf. 45.

866. **tristis**, 'surly.' Cf. 79 note.

tenax, sc. *rei*, 'close-fisted.'

The original of the line is in Menander,

ἐγὼ δ' ἄγροικος, ἐργάτης, σκυθρός, πικρός,
φειδωλός.

867. **ibi**, sc. *in matrimonio*. The troubles of the married man were

I

made the subject of frequent jests on the Roman stage. Cf. 28-34, 43-4, and especially the character of Nausistrata in the Phormio.

868. heia autem, 'but heigh-ho:' probably meant as a translation of ἀλλ' εἶα. The Latin interjection is more elastic than the Greek. For while εἶα is confined to stimulating exclamations, 'come,' 'up,' 'away,' etc., *heia*, also written *eia*, may express joy, surprise, admiration, strong affirmation, ironical doubt, weariness, as here, and so on.

870. exacta aetate, 'at the end of my life.'

fructi. In early Latin the gen. of this declension ended in *-uis*, e.g. Haut. 287 *anuis*. This was contracted (*a*) into *-ûs*, (*b*) into *-i*, the lightly pronounced *s* being first dropped, and then *-ui* shortened to *-i*. Only the form in *-ûs* is used by Augustan authors, but Ennius, Lucretius, Plautus, and Terence employ both forms side by side. We find in Terence *adventi*, *domi*, *fructi*, *ornati*, *quaesti*, *tumulti*. Neither Plautus nor Terence ever write *domûs* as the genitive. With *hoc fructi* compare *hoc villi* 786.

871. patria. Cf. 74 note.

potitur. In Terence *potior* is found three times constructed with an accusative, once with an ablative; cf. 876, Phor. 469, 830: in Plautus with the acc., abl., or gen. Ovid Her. 14. 113 once writes *potītur*, otherwise the *i* is always found short.

872. illi credunt ... Demea ignores the fact, which possibly Micio's nonchalance may have concealed from him, that Aeschinus kept his relations with Pamphila a profound secret from his adopted father.

874. illum ut vivat optant = *ut ille vivat optant*. Donatus notices this as an archaism.

scilicet, 'no doubt.'

875. eductos. Cf. 48 note.

876. potitur. Cf. 871 note.

877. possiem = *possim*. Cf. 83 note.

878. quando hoc provocat, 'since he (sc. Micio) challenges me to it.' Cf. προκαλεῖσθαι.

hoc, archaic for *huc*, as *istoc* and *istuc*. *Hoc* = *huc* is not uncommon in Plautus, is used also by Terence Eun. 394, 501, and by Vergil A. 8. 423.

879. magni fieri, 'to be made much of.' The Calliopian MSS. give *magni pendi*.

880. posteriores, sc. *partes*, 'I will not play second fiddle.' Cf. Hor. Sat. 1. 9. 46 *posset qui ferre secundas*.

881. deerit, sc. *res*, 'the property will not stand it.' Demea's natural parsimony reasserts itself for a moment; but he consoles himself with the reflection that the money will last for his time.

Act V. Scene 2 [5].

Demea at once begins to practise his new affability on Syrus.

883. **quid fit? quid agitur?** Cf. 266 note.

886. **servom haud inliberalem**, 'by no means a bad slave.' Cf. Andr. 38 *propterea quod servibas liberaliter;* supra 57 note.

887. **lubens bene faxim**, 'I should be delighted to do you a good turn.' For *faxim* cf. 209 note.

atqui, etc. This asseveration is drawn forth by the manifest incredulity of Syrus.

Act V. Scene 3 [6].

Demea continues his clumsy compliments to Geta.

889. **huc ad hos proviso**, 'I am coming to these gentlemen out here (*pointing*) to see.' Cf. 549.

890. **eccum.** Cf. 260 note.

sies. Cf. 83 note.

891. **qui vocare?** 'What is your name?' *Qui* is abl. = *quo nomine*. Cf. 179 note.

893. **servos spectatus satis**, 'a slave of proved fidelity.' Notice the alliteration.

895. **siquid usus venerit**, 'if any opportunity occurs:' *siquid* being used adverbially, 'if at all.'

896. **lubens bene faxim.** Notice Demea's poverty of polite phrases. Cf. 887.

897. **quom.** Cf. 39 note.

898. **primulum.** Cf. 289 note. Notice the alliteration.

Act V. Scene 4 [7].

Demea electrifies Aeschinus by hurrying on the marriage preparations, and by professions of lavish cordiality towards Sostrata and her household.

899. **occidunt me**, 'they weary me to death.'

equidem, so A, the other MSS. *quidem*. *Equidem* is compounded of the particle *e*, which we also find in *ecastor* and *edepol*. It does not stand for *ego quidem*, and is sometimes found with the second or third person, though more common with the first. Cf. Eun. 956 *atque equidem orante, ut ne id faceret, Thaide*. Ritschl expressed a strong opinion (Prol. 76 sqq.) that it was only used with the first person in Plautus, but has since retracted; see his note on Pl. Trin. 352, published at Leipsic, 1871.

sanctas, 'ceremonious.'

116   *ADELPHI.*

901. **tu hic eras?** 'were you here?' i.e. when I made my last remark. In English we should more naturally use the present; the imperfect here may be an imitation of the so-called 'immediate' aorist in Greek.

905. **hymenaeum,** 'the nuptial song.' Songs were sung by hired musicians during the wedding ceremonies, and after their conclusion at the door of the bridal chamber; these latter being called *Epithalamia.* Cf. Catul. 62. 5.

906. **vin** = *visne.* Cf. 969.

missa haec face, 'away with these things.' This is a common phrase in Terence, e. g. 991, Andr. 680, 833.

face. Cf. 241 note.

907. **turbas,** i. e. the wedding procession, which escorted the bride to her husband's house.

lampadas, referring to the torch of thorn or pine-wood carried by a boy in the procession, and to the illumination of the house at the wedding-feast.

908 This line shows that Micio and Sostrata were supposed to be occupying adjoining houses in the same street.

909. **quantum potest.** Cf. 350.

hac, sc. *via.*

910. **traduce.** Cf. 241 note.

911. **euge,** 'bravo;' Gr. εὖγε.

lepidissume, 'most charming.' Cf. 966.

913. **quid mea,** sc. *refert?* Cf. 881.

914–5. **iube ... minas,** 'bid that nabob pay down twenty minae on the spot.'

iube dinumeret. Both Plautus and Terence sometimes construct *iubere* with the subjunctive. e. g. Eun. 691, Haut. 737.

ille Babylo, i. e. Micio. The luxury and extravagance of Babylonians seem to have been proverbial, and Demea gives his brother this nick-name on account of his prodigality. Twenty minae had been the sum already paid by Micio for the music-girl (cf. 191, 369); Demea now, with mischievous glee, bids him disburse the like amount for the expenses of the wedding. Babylo is ἅπαξ λεγόμενον. Some have thought Babylo to be a steward of Micio or Demea; but the presence of *ille* puts this out of the question.

Line 914 is the last now legible in A. Of the three last leaves only the margins with some isolated letters remain.

916. **dirue,** sc. *maceriam.* Cf. 908.

917. **tu illas abi et traduce** = *tu abi et illas traduce,* a case of *hyperbaton* or σύγχυσις.

918. **quom te video.** Cf. 139 note.

919. **ex animo.** Cf. 72 note.

factum velle. Cf. 165 *nollem factum*. Translate, 'since I see that you befriend our family so heartily.' Cf. Phor. 787.

dignos, i. e. the family.

921. **hac,** sc. *via*. Cf. 909.

922. **nil enim.** Cf. 168 note.

923. **eccum.** Cf. 260 note.

ACT V. SCENE 5 [8].

Micio has found Syrus pulling down the garden-wall, by Demea's order, as the slave alleges. In utter astonishment he comes out to discover what it all means. Demea at once shows how enlarged his views have become. He insists that his bachelor brother must marry Sostrata and reward Hegio by the present of a nice little farm, and, backed up by Aeschinus, actually extorts a reluctant consent from the bewildered Micio.

925. **ego vero iubeo** = καὶ δὴ κελεύω, 'Yes, I do order it.'

928. **nobis decet.** Cf. 491 note.

929. **postea.** Cf. 529 note.

931. **parere ... non potest.** Demea would not have urged the match, had there been any chance of children to inherit Micio's property instead of Aeschinus.

iam diu haec per annos non potest. For this use of the present compare the French idiom, '*depuis longtemps elle ne peut pas. ...*'

934. **autem.** Cf. 185 note, 935.

ineptis. Terence only uses the verb here and in Phor. 420.

si tu sis homo. Cf. 107 note.

935. **asine.** Cf. Haut. 877 *quae sunt dicta in stulto, caudex, stipes, asinus, plumbeus. . . .*

937. **aufer.** The exact meaning of this word cannot be certainly determined. Donatus says *aufer vel te vel manum*, i. e. either 'away with you,' or 'hands off.' The latter interpretation is dramatically probable, as may be seen from the stage directions. On the other hand *aufer te* is used twice by Plautus, while *aufer manum* is not found elsewhere. Either *te* or *manum* is more probable than *nugas*, as suggested by Lewis and Short.

da veniam, 'grant this favour,' as in 942, and frequently.

939. **estis auctores** = *suadetis*, and so is followed by an acc. as though the phrase were really transitive. Cf. Pl. Poen. I. 3. 1 *quid nunc mihi es auctor, Milphio?* supra 617.

940. promisti. Cf. 561 note.

autem. Cf. 185 note.

de te is much more forcible than *de tuo*, seeing that Aeschinus had been liberal enough, according to his own account, to offer Micio himself to Sostrata.

941. age. Cf. 271 note.

942. non. Cf. 94 note.

943. vis, 'downright violence.'

age, prolixe, 'come, be generous.' *Prolixe*, an adverb.

946-7. Both the readings and the distribution of the words among the speakers are uncertain. The text keeps as closely as possible to the MSS. In 946 *confit* is admitted for *fit* on the authority of Donatus, an additional syllable being necessary for the metre. In 947 *cognatus* and *his est* have been transposed for the same reasons. No MS. marks a change of speaker before *merito* or *quid nunc* or *Hegio*. All MSS. assign *verum quid*, etc. to Demea. Bentley conjectured,

DE. *Merito tuo te amo ; verum*—MI. *Quid?* DE. *Ego dicam, hoc cum fit quod volo.*

MI. *Quid nunc? quid restat?* DE. *Hegio hic est his cognatus proximus.*

He has been followed with some variations by many editors, but the text of the MSS. gives a very good sense. With *quid nunc* understand *est*.

948. adfinis, sc. by the marriage of Pamphila and Aeschinus.

nos facere decet. Cf. 491 note.

949. agelli paululum, 'a little bit of a farm.' Here and in 650 most editors alter the MSS. reading *paululum* to *paulum* on account of the roughness of the metre.

locitas foras, 'you often let.' The frequentative termination probably implies that the farm in question was so poor that no tenant stopped on it long.

950. qui. Cf. 179 note. 'Let us allow him to have the use of it.'

autem. Cf. 185 note.

951. huic, i.e. Pamphila. Demea points to Sostrata's house.

952. non = *nonne*. Cf. 94 note. 'Do I not now appropriate that saying which ...' Or *non meum* may be closely connected, 'That saying is none of mine which ...' This, however, makes *facio* difficult.

953. dixti. Cf. 561 note.

dudum, 'just now,' i.e. 833-4. *Dudum* can also mean 'some time ago.' In Pl. Trin. 608 *quam dudum* = 'how long ago.' Cf. Phor. 459 *incertior sum multo quam dudum*.

954. senecta. This form is ἅπαξ λεγόμενον in Terence, but is often found in Plautus alongside of *senectus*. It is probably an adjective

agreeing with *aetas*, which is frequently expressed in the phrase *senecta aetate*.

956. quid istic? Cf. 133 note. The MSS. give *istuc*, but the phrase is so common that the change is justified.

956–7. As these verses stand in the MSS. they are *senarii*. As 934–955 and 958 are *octonarii* (iambic), some editors assume *lacunae* in 956–7.

958. suo sibi gladio hunc iugulo, 'I hoist him with his own petard.' *Sibi* throws additional emphasis on *suo*, 'his own particular.' For a scene ending with a broken line see 81 note.

ACT V. SCENE 6 [9].

Demea completes the discomfiture of Micio by prevailing on him to manumit Syrus and his wife, besides advancing them money to make a start in life on their own account. His bewildered brother appeals to him for an explanation, whereupon Demea, in his true character, points the moral of the Play and the curtain falls [1].

959. frugi homo 's, 'yon are a useful fellow.'

frugi is really a *dativus commodi* of the obsolete *frux*. Practically it is used as an indeclinable adjective, in Terence applied usually to slaves. Cf. 982.

960. The order is *iudico aequom esse Syrum fieri liberum*.

962. usque a pueris; cf. 41 *iam inde ab adulescentia*. Syrus was the παιδαγωγός.

963. quae potui. Cf. 423 note.

964. haec, nom. in apposition to the following infinitives, repeated in 966.

obsonare cum fide, 'to be a trusty caterer.'

965. de die, 'at noon.' Cf. 841 *de nocte*. To dine early was a sign of luxury and dissipation. Cf. Liv. 23. 8. The usual hour for *cena* was 3.0 p.m.

966. lepidum caput. Cf. 261, 911.

968. alii, sc. *servi*.

969. hic, i.e. Aeschinus.

vin. Cf. 906.

972. perpetuom, 'complete,' lit. without a break in it.

---

[1] In Roman theatres the curtain was lowered (*aulaea premere*) to the floor or perhaps drawn under the stage at the commencement of an Act, and raised again at the conclusion (*aulaea tollere*). Cf. Hor. Ep. 2. 1. 189 *quattuor aut plures aulaea premuntur in horas*, Verg. G. 3..25 *purpurea intexti tollant aulaea Britanni*.

973. Phrygiam. It was customary at Rome to name slaves according to their nationality, e. g. Syrus, Geta, etc.

974. tuo, sc. Demea ; **huius,** sc. Aeschinus.

976. emitti, sc. *manu,* 'that she should be freed.'

979. processisti pulchre, 'you have got on finely.'

980. tuom officium, i. e. as *Patronus.*

prae manu, 'in hand.'

981. dederis. A double protasis with the verbs in different tenses, as here, is rare, though each tense is the natural one in its own clause.

unde utatur, '*de quo usum fructum capiat*' (Donat.), 'to live upon.'

istoc vilius, sc. *dabo,* 'less than that,' snapping his fingers, or making some equivalent gesture.

982. frugi homo est. Cf. 959.

983. festivissime. Cf. 261, 986.

985. prolubium [*pro-lubet*], 'whim,' a word not found in any classical author. This line is apparently adapted from a verse of Caecilius,

Quod prolubium, quae voluptas, quae te lactat largitas?

A very early variant is *proluvium,* explained by Nonius as 'extravagance' (*profusio*), found in B C² D G and read by Donatus, Nonius, and Servius. *Proluvium* is certainly easier than *prolubium* in this context, but the parallel passage in Caecilius is too close to be disregarded, especially when we consider that *prolubium* might easily be turned into *proluvium,* while the reverse could hardly take place. Translate, 'what means this new whim of yours, this sudden liberality?'

986. quod ... putant. This clause is explanatory of *id.* Translate, ' your reputation with your nephews for good-nature and good-fellowship.'

987. ex vera vita, 'from integrity of life.' This sense of *verus* is not rare; cf. Andr. 629 *ah! id est verum?* Cic. Leg. 2. 5. 11 *quod est rectum verum quoque est.*

adeo. Cf. 629 note, 989.

989. vobis ... Aeschine. Cf. Verg. A. 1. 140 *vestras, Eure, domos,* 9. 525 *Vos, O Calliope.* . . . The figure by which all are understood though only one is mentioned is called *Synecdoche,* Roby § 950.

990. iusta iniusta, acc. of respect, *vobis* being understood after *obsequor.* Translate, 'because I do not humour you in absolutely everything in every way, right or wrong.'

991. missa facio, 'I wash my hands of it.' Cf. 906 note.

quod vobis lubet. This verb is not rare with a personal construction in Plautus and Terence.

992-5. Translate, ' but if in those things wherein youth makes you short-sighted, over-eager, and thoughtless, you rather choose to have reproof, correction, and indulgence at the proper times, here am I at your service.'

The MSS. insert *me* after *corrigere*. This is almost certainly a gloss, as it not only spoils the metre, but also the climax *ecce me*. The infinitives *reprehendere*, etc., grammatically require an acc. *aliquem* to be understood before them; but this was perhaps intentionally omitted in order to make the expression as impersonal as possible.

in loco. Cf. 216 note.

996. quid facto opus est. Cf. 195, 335 notes.

997. habeat, sc. *psaltriam*.

Cantor. Between two or more of the Acts of a Roman Comedy it was the custom to introduce a lyrical monologue (*canticum*) with a flute accompaniment. Sometimes, as in the Trinummus, this *canticum* was made an integral part of the play, but more commonly it was performed by a *Cantor*, who also came forward at the end of the play, and said to the audience *plaudite*; cf. Hor. A. P. 155 *donec Cantor* '*vos plaudite*' *dicat*. In all Terence's plays the MSS. mark the Cantor by Ω. The actors are often indicated by letters of the Greek alphabet in the order of their appearance on the stage, and Ω became naturally appropriated to the Cantor, because he always came on last. The Cantor in this play is Flaccus, slave of Claudius, cf. Didascalia.

INDEX TO NOTES.

References are to the number of the lines. Words distinguished by an asterisk are ἅπαξ λεγόμενα. When the same word has been noted more than once, but in different case, person, tense, etc., the references will be found under the form which occurs first; and when the same point occurs several times references are given in the place where it is first noted.

A.

a me, 788.
ab re, 830.
abduce, 482.
abi, 220, 703.
Ablative of quality, 161, 442.
abripiere, 181.
abs, 254.
absolvitote, 282.
Accusative and Infinitive (*in exclamations*), etc., 38.
— (*of exclamation*), 304, 783.
— (*of limitation*), 423.
ad Dianae, 582.
Adelphoe, note on Title.
adeo, 629.
adnumeravit, 369.
adsentandi, 270.
adsero manu, 194.
advocatum, 646.
Aemilio Paulo, note on Title.
aequanimitas, 24.
Affirmative phrases, 287, 543.
age, 271.
aibas, 561.
alienam, 672.
aliquoi rei, 358.
Alliteration, 1, 11, 134, 160, 182, 211-2, 322, 335, 490, 893, 898.
Ambivius Turpio, note on Title.
an, 136.
angiportum, 576.

animam recipe, 324.
animi, 610.
animo obsequi, 33.
antiqua, 442.
anulus, 347.
anus, 646.
articulo, 229.
Assonance, 57, 127, 160, 211-2, 322.
atque (*adversative*), 40.
Attraction (*inverse*), 807.
auctor, 671.
auctores estis (*with Accusative*), 939.
aufer, 937.
auferent, 454.
aut, 396.
autem, 185.
auxili, 300.
auxiliarier, 273.

B.

*Babylo, 914.
bellissumum, 590.
bonus, 476.

C.

cantites, 750.
Cantor, 997.
capite in terram statuerem, 316.
captus, 480.
caput, 568.

INDEX TO NOTES.

cautio, 421.
cave dixeris, 458.
cedo, 123.
clam, 71.
clanculum, 52.
Claudi, note on Title.
claudier, 607.
coeperet, 397.
Commorientis, 7.
compos animi, 310.
constabilisses, 771.
consuevit, 666.
consulis, 127.
'*Contamination*,' 5, 10, heading to Act ii. sc. 1.
contra, 44, 50.
conveniunt, 59.
coram, 484.
credo (*parenthetical*), 79.
crepuit, 264.
Ctesiphonem, 252.
cyathos, 591.

D.

Dative (*ethic*), 61.
de die, 965.
de lucro, 817.
de meo, 117.
de nocte, 841.
debacchatus es, 184.
decet, 491.
dedisti, 450.
defervisse, 152.
defrudet, 246.
defunctum sit, 507.
dementia, 390.
demum, 255.
deorsum, 573.
designavit, 87.
di vostram fidem, 381.
Didascalia, note on Title.
Diminutive termination, 566, 647, 949.
Diphili, 6.
dis (=dives), 770.
discidit, 559.
dispergat, 317.

disperii, 355.
disrumpor, 369.
Dittography, 209.
dolet, 272.
dudum, 953.
dum, 196.

E.

eccum, 260.
edepol, 289.
eduxi, 48.
ei (=hei), 124.
ellum, 260.
em, 169, 537.
emergi, 302.
emitti, 976.
enarramus, 365.
enim, 168.
equidem, 899.
ergo, 172.
erili filiae, 301.
erratio, 580.
esse (*ellipse of*), 13.
euge, 911.
ex animo, 72.
ex sententia, 371.
excurso spatio, 860.
experiar, 350.
exporge, 839.
expostules, 595.
extulit, 11.

F.

face, 241.
faciam (*with Abl.*), 611.
faeneraret, 219.
familia, 297.
faxim, } 209.
faxo, }
fert, 53, 730.
fervit, 534.
festivom caput, 261.
fide optuma, 161.
fit sedulo, 413.
flagitium, 101.
foras, 109.
foris, 264.

INDEX TO NOTES. 125

fructi, 870.
frugi, 959.
functus est, 464.
funeralibus, note on Title.
Future Perfect (use of), 127, 437.

G.

genere, 297.
Genitive (in -i for -ii), 300.
— *(in -i for -us)*, 870.
— *(in -um for -orum)*, 411, 793.
— *(of price)*, 163.
Gerundive in -undus, 193.
grandem, 673.

H.

haberet, 365.
hariolor, 202.
heia, 868.
hem, 260.
Hiatus, 183, 304, 336, 574, 604, 697, 767.
hilarem, 287.
hinc, 361.
hinc illinc, 673.
hoc (=huc), 878.
homines nobiles, 15.
homo, 107, 579.
humane, 145.
hymenaeum, 905.
Hyperbaton, 917.

I.

ierant, 27.
ii, 23.
ilicet, 791.
ilico *(of place)*, 156.
illi (=illic), 116.
in loco, 216.
in medio, 479.
in otio, 20.
inde, 47.
Indicative (after quom *causal)*, 139.
— *(in dependent sentences)*, 195.
indicente, 507.
indicio erit, 4.

indignum, 166.
ineptis, 934.
Infinitive (in indignant expressions), 38, 237, 330.
— *(Historic)*, 45.
— *(after* videre), 95.
— *(in* -ier), 200.
— *(Pres. for Fut. after verbs of promising, etc.)*, 203, 224.
infitias ibit, 339.
inliberale, 449.
inpertiri, 320.
inpotentiam, 607.
inruat se, 550.
insuerit, 55.
Interrogative particle omitted, 136, 619.
ipsus, 328.
ire video, 360.
istoc vilius, 981.
istocine, 732.
iube *(with Subjunctive)*, 914.
ingulo, 958.
iurgabit, 80.

L.

lacum, 583.
lampadas, 907.
lautum, 425.
lectulos in sole, 585.
liberali causa, 194.
liberos, 57.
locitas, 949.
loris liber, 182.
lubuit, 766, 991.
luci, 841.
lupus in fabula, 537.

M.

male, 523.
malevoli, 15.
mallem potius, 222.
malo, 69, 554.
malum, 544.
mastigia, 781.
mea tu, 289.
medium, 316.

Menandru, note on Title.
Mileti, 654.
militatum, 385.
minis, 191, 370.
minume gentium, 341.
misere, 522.
missa face, 906.
modo, 289.
modos fecit, note on Title.
morem gestum oportuit, 214.
morigeratus, 218.

N.

nam (*intensive*), 168.
-ne (*in exclamations*), 38, 304.
-ne (=nonne), 83.
-ne (=num), 676.
-ne (*omitted*), 136.
ne (*with Pres. Imperative*), 279.
ne (*affirmative particle*), 441.
ne dicam dolo, 375.
ne tam quidem, 278.
nequit, 76.
nescio quid, 79.
nil quicquam, 366.
nisi, 153.
nisi si, 593.
nollem factum, 165.
non (=nonne), 94.
nonne, 660.
norimus, 270.
numquam, 98.
numquam hodie, 551.
numquid vis, 247.
nunciam, 156.

O.

obnuntio, 547.
obsequor, 990.
observari, 2.
obtine, 812, 814.
occulte fert, 328.
ohe iam, 723.

olfecissem, 397.
opus, 335.
os praebui, 215.

P.

*parasitaster, 779.
Parenthetical phrases, 79.
paternum, 74.
patrissas, 564.
patrium, 74.
paucis, 806.
paululus, 779.
peccato, 174.
penes vos, 388.
pepulisti, 638.
per- (*prefix*), 393.
perbenigne, 702.
perpetuom, 972.
perreptavi, 715.
pie, 459.
pistrilla, 584.
placabilius, 608.
platea, 574.
Pleonastic phrases, 224.
plus, 199.
poeta, 1.
Polysyndeton, 64.
postea, 529.
potest, 302, 350, 357.
potin, 539.
potis, 344.
potitur, 871.
praeter, 258.
Present tense (*noteworthy uses of*), 339, 435, 931.
primarum artium principem, 259.
primulum, 289.
pro divom fidem, 746.
*prodeambulare, 766.
produxe, 561.
prolixe, 943.
prolubium, 985.
propter, 169, 576.
proviso, 889.

INDEX TO NOTES.   127

pudet, 84, 683.
pugnaveris, 843.
pultare, 633.
putemus, 796.

Q.

quaere rem, 482.
quaerito, 81.
quam (*with Superlative*), 501.
quantum potest, 350.
quantus quantu's, 394.
qui (*Abl.*), 179.
qui (*causal*), 268.
quid=aliquid, 443.
quid agitur, 266.
quid ais, 556.
quid fit, 266.
quid istic, 133.
quid ni, 466.
quin, 262.
quisque, 399.
quivis (=quovis), 254.
quod, 162, 296, 299.
quom, 18.
quom (*causal with Ind.*), 139.
quom maxime, 518.

R.

rapere in peiorem partem, 3.
redducas, 830.
refrixerit, 233.
regnum, 175.
rei, 95, 220.
restim ductans, 752.
ruerem, 319.

S.

Salus, 761.
sapientia, 427.
Sarranis, note on Title.
Scansion (peculiarities of), 10, 22, 25, 27, 35, 72, 86, 106, 156, 173, 192, 255, 260.
scibo, 360.
scire est, 828.
scriptura, 1.

scrupulum, 228.
senecta, 954.
serva, 172.
servolorum, 27, 566.
si dis placet, 476.
sic (δεικτικῶς), 305.
siet, 83.
siit (=sivit), 104.
silicernium, 587.
simile (*with Genitive*), 96.
sine superbia, 21.
siquid (*adverbial*), 895.
sis (=si vis), 766.
socordem, 695.
sodes, 578.
soli, 34.
somnium, 395.
sorte, 243.
Sostrata, 343.
spero (*parenthetical*), 226, 411.
subducta, 855.
Subject (ellipse of), 24, 52, 77, 924.
Subjunctive (in questions), 84, 261.
—.(*Imperfect for Pluperfect*), 106.
sumamus, 287.
suom (=suorum), 411.
sursum, 574.
Syncopated forms, 55, 104, 209, 561.
Synecdoche, 989.
Synizesis, 72, 79, 160, 166, 561.

T.

tacito est opus, 341.
tamen, 110.
tandem, 276.
tantidem, 200.
tantillum, 563.
tanto nequior, 528.
tenax, 866.
Tense (change of), 603, 981.
tesseris, 739.
Tmesis, 662.
tollebas, 809.
tradier, 200.

traduce, 910.
tribulis, 439.
tristem, 79, 866.
tristitiem, 269.
turba, 615.

V.

ubi (=*since*), 82.
ultro, 472.
unde, 413.
unumquicquid, 590.
usque, 559.
usque ad, 90.
usus, 429.
ut (*with imprecations*), 713.
ut ne (= ut non), 625.

utantur, 815, 981.
utrum . . ne, 382.

V (CONSONANTAL).

velim, 519.
vendundam, 193.
vera vita, 987.
Verbal Substantives, 421.
verbum, 803.
verum, 543.
vestitu (*dative*), 63.
viderit, 437, 538.
*villi, 786.
vin, 906.
vis, 490.
viso, 549.

THE END.

www.ingramcontent.com/pod-product-compliance
Lightning Source LLC
Chambersburg PA
CBHW030257170426
43202CB00009B/784